ACCESS®

Cover: Brazil's Valber attempts to block a shot from Argentina's Gabriel Batistuta in a 1993 Copa América match in Guayaquil, Ecuador.

Introduction

"Soccer is not a matter of life and death, it's much more important than that." So said the famous English coach **Bill Shankly.** His passion for the sport is shared by millions of people around the world, many of whom consider soccer a religion, something to be worshiped every waking hour of the day. Presidents, rock stars, and even the Pope number among its fans. During the 1986 World Cup finals, the pontiff, a self-confessed soccer fanatic, cut short a visit to a Rome church because it coincided with television coverage of a crucial match between Italy and Austria and he did not want "to compete with the national duty to be sitting in front of the television."

The impact of what the legendary Brazilian soccer star **Pelé** once described as "the world's most beautiful game" manifests itself differently in every country. In Saudi Arabia, officials in flowing robes discuss the finer points of the game with track-suited players at state-of-the-art, multimillion-dollar stadiums. More than 100,000 people once assembled at Abidjan Airport to greet the victorious Ivory Coast team just back from winning the African Nations Cup in Senegal, and one million spectators lined the official victory parade route. Add to these images the picture of kids playing Saturday morning soccer in Seattle, St. Louis, Baltimore, or anywhere in small town America, now that the sport has firmly established itself in the United States.

Soccer's Worldwide Popularity

The universal appeal of soccer is best illustrated by the fact that 141 nations officially entered the qualifying draw for the 1994 World Cup—an impressive 25-percent increase over the number of entries for the previous World Cup. The draw took place in New York on 8 December 1991, barely 18 months after the end of the last World Cup. Even though three countries—Cuba, Western Samoa, and Sierra Leone—subsequently withdrew without even kicking a ball, a record-breaking 138 nations still officially entered the competition.

The first qualifying match pitted the Dominican Republic against Puerto Rico. Some 582 matches and almost two years later—culminating in Argentina's 1-0 defeat of Australia—the number of countries to join defending champion Germany and the United States, the host nation, for the finals, had been whittled down to an elite group of 22.

Soccer draws a worldwide television audience larger than that of any other sport. For the month-long 1990 World Cup, held in Italy, television viewers tuned in 27 billion times, nearly double the 15 billion times viewers watched the 1992 Barcelona Summer Olympics. The final between West Germany and Argentina accounted for more than 1 billion viewers—a figure equivalent to about a fifth of the world's entire population, almost four times the 253 million who watched the 1993 Super Bowl. Even the draw for the 1990 soccer finals attracted 67 million more worldwide viewers than the 1993 Super Bowl. A grand total of 167 countries carried television coverage of the 1990 World Cup, with the average broadcasting time per country being an astounding 88 hours.

Soccer is played in just about every country in the world, and in most of them—the United States and Canada being notable exceptions—it's far and away the number one sport. **The Fédération Internationale de Football Association,** soccer's international governing body (known the world over by its acronym **FIFA**), has 180 member countries, putting it on a par with the United Nations.

According to **FIFA,** more than 150 million people in every corner of the globe (including 10 million women) are officially registered soccer players, and in the course of a year, one million referees officiate some 20 million matches.

Soccer in the United States

In a 1990 article listing the 10 most important skills Americans would need for the '90s, *USA Today* proclaimed: "You will have to learn a new sport: Football. Soccer, as we call it. If you continue to think **Diego Maradona** is a South American wine, you'll be the laughingstock of any cocktail party. Learn everything you can about it, now that the U.S. team will be in competition." *People* magazine also predicted greater visibility for soccer in the United States during the '90s in a special 1990 issue: "Almost 13 million U.S. kids play soccer, and its version of Little League has exploded fifteen fold since 1975. Yet most grown-ups couldn't tell a corner kick from a corn chip."

Soccer is unquestionably the fastest growing sport in the United States. A national 1993 survey by the **Soccer Industry Council of America (SICA)** revealed that 15.2 million Americans played the game at least once during the previous year. The 6.8 million players under

12 years of age established soccer as the second most popular sport among kids in that age group, after basketball (with 8.9 million participants), but ahead of softball, touch football, baseball, and volleyball.

The most explosive growth has taken place within the independent youth soccer leagues—scores of youngsters can now be seen on soccer fields all over the country. In 1992, more than two-and-a-quarter million children were officially registered with three principal nationwide organizations: the **American Youth Soccer Organization,** the **United States Youth Soccer Association,** and the **Soccer Association for Youth**—a healthy five-percent increase over the previous year's figures and a whopping 84-percent increase over the number who played 10 years ago. Only in the country's inner-city neighborhoods has soccer yet to make an impact, but even there some major inroads are beginning, thanks to such programs as **Soccer in the Streets** and **Soccer Start.**

Why has soccer become so phenomenally popular among children in the United States? The most commonly advanced reasons are that equipment costs are low; short, lightweight players can do just as well as tall, heavyweight players in almost every position, so size isn't much of a factor; every player can get equally involved because the sport isn't dominated by several key positions; and the risk of getting injured is relatively low.

At the high school level, more schools added a boys' soccer program during the 1991-92 season than any other sport, although soccer still lags behind football, basketball, baseball, and outdoor track-and-field in total high school participants. The numbers are even more dramatic among high school girls: soccer vaulted from the 12th most popular sport in 1978-79 to sixth place in 1991-92. The same steady progress is being made at the college level, where the number of **National Collegiate Athletic Association (NCAA)** and **National Association of Intercollegiate Athletics (NAIA)** varsity men's soccer teams has now overtaken the number of varsity football teams. Even adult participation is on the increase; more than 140,000 players were registered with the **United States Amateur Soccer Association** for the 1991-92 season, representing an almost 50-percent increase over the 1985-86 season.

For obvious reasons, observers tend to make comparisons between soccer and football. The **National Sporting Goods Association** has determined that it costs $276 to outfit a football player compared to $54 for a soccer player. Furthermore, the average football roster is twice as long as that of soccer—in other words, most football players warm the bench for half of each game. An analysis by *The Wall Street Journal* revealed that about 377,000 of the million or so youngsters playing football at some 15,000 U.S. high schools will be injured each year, 60,000 of them seriously, and approximately 15,000 of them will require surgery. This may explain why more than 1,500 high school football teams folded in the 1980s, while the number of high school soccer teams grew by 2,000 during that period, according to a 1990 article in **USA Today.**

Some prominent football personalities have been won over by soccer. "I think soccer is the best sport available in America for youngsters," says **Tom Landry,** the former Dallas Cowboys coach and chairman of a group that successfully lobbied to get Dallas selected as one of the U.S. sites for the 1994 World Cup. "Football is just too tough on youngsters—children still growing. The growing bones are not ready for the impact. Soccer lets children develop coordination and physical attributes without taking a pounding. It's a great sport for youth."

When it comes to soccer's visibility as a major spectator sport, however, the United States still has a way to go. A *USA Today* study, published in 1990, showed that of the 12 million kids under the age of 19 playing soccer in this country, only seven percent said that it was their favorite sport, ranking it behind higher visibility games such as basketball, baseball, and football.

The main problem is America's lack of exposure to world-class soccer. Since the demise of the North American Soccer League in 1985, there has been no full-time professional soccer league in this country. Many of the best American players—in search of lucrative contracts and a more competitive standard of soccer—graduate from high school, college, and youth league ranks, only to find themselves forced to play abroad. In recent years, **U.S. Soccer,** America's governing body, has tried to counter this exodus by offering year-round professional contracts to members of the national team, but most of the country's top players are still joining foreign leagues.

Soccer has also not made much of an impact on U.S. television compared to other major sports. The U.S. share of the gigantic one billion television viewers for the 1990 World Cup final was a paltry 570,000. Instead of coverage on a national network, as there had been with the 1982 and 1986 competitions, the 1990 finals were televised by Turner Network Television, a cable station with access to only 45 million U.S. households.

However, in the late 1980s and early 1990s, as the United States prepared to host the 1994 World Cup, some encouraging developments took place. Support of the U.S. national team dramatically improved as the team itself became more competitive. Many records were set around the country, including the first $1 million in gate revenue in U.S. history for the 1993 U.S. Cup match in Detroit between the United States and Germany.

The increasing ethnic diversity of the United States is probably a factor contributing to newfound interest in soccer. During the 1984 Summer Olympics in Los Angeles, for instance, 1.4 million spectators came to watch the soccer tournament—more than for any other sport during the Games. Over 100,000 fans crammed into the Rose Bowl for both the Gold Medal and the Bronze Medal matches. The lure of the 1994 World Cup in nine U.S. cities proved irresistible as well. All 3.6 million tickets were sold for the 1994 finals, creating a sellout for every single one of the 52 matches, the first time this has ever happened in World Cup history.

Equipment

One of the reasons for soccer's burgeoning popularity in recent years is that it costs so little to outfit players compared to equipping them for other team sports such as football, baseball, and hockey. Official soccer regulations list "a jersey or shirt, shorts, stockings, shinguards, and footwear" as the only compulsory equipment—that and a ball, of course.

Not that it's impossible to spend some significant change on equipment, if you're so inclined. In fact, soccer has progressed considerably from the days of baggy shorts drooping to the knees, heavy shirts with buttoned collars, bulky shinguards, and metal-toe-capped shoes with leather cleats nailed to the soles. Today's manufacturers offer sleek, sophisticated clothing at equally sophisticated prices, but it's still possible to outfit an aspiring young star for as little as $50.

The Ball

The world's first soccer ball was probably a human skull. According to one account, members of a tribe living in central England in the third century started kicking around the skulls of former Roman soldiers. Some 800 years later, evidence shows, a London tribe celebrated a gruesome victory against Viking invaders by cutting off the Scandinavian leader's head and playing an early form of soccer with it.

In medieval times, players punted a ball made of leather stuffed with animal hair. When the English sport reached America in the 17th century, the colonists rolled deer hair into a soft ball and covered it with deerskin. By the middle of the 19th century, American Ivy League soccer players were using leather balls filled with paper, leaves, and cloth.

In Britain, the early ball was comprised of eight leather panels with an inflatable bladder (rubber bag) inside. But after a fair amount of kicking, the leather panels would stretch, producing a misshapen sphere with all kinds of bulges. On wet fields, the ball would become heavy and waterlogged, so it was literally a pain to play it with one's head.

Today's soccer balls have a plastic casing to repel water and 32 stitched panels that prevent stretching. Sialkot, a city in northeastern Pakistan, produces more than 35 million soccer balls each year, which meets most of the world's needs. Balls now come in three main sizes:

Ball Size	Circumference	Weight	Players
3	23.5 to 26"	10.5 to 12oz.	Children ages 3-7
4	25 to 26"	11.5 to 13.5oz.	Children ages 8-11
5	27 to 28"	14 to 16oz.	High school, college, & professional teams

Keeping a ball properly inflated is important. In professional play, the required pressure is nine to 10.5 pounds per square inch at sea level. Soccer balls cost as little as $10 to $15 for the basic variety, to around $100 for official World Cup balls.

But not having a regulation ball hasn't deterred many diehard players. As a youngster, Brazilian soccer superstar **Pelé** played on the streets of Bauru, Brazil, with a bundle of rags wrapped in string, and his compatriots still amuse themselves on the beach by dribbling grapefruit.

Travails of a Trophy

The World Cup statuette itself has led a charmed life. The original trophy, a gold cup designed by French sculptor **Abel Lafleur**, was named after fellow Frenchman **Jules Rimet**, who became president of **FIFA** in 1921. At the onset of World War II, two Italian soccer officials, fearing that the Jules Rimet Trophy could fall in the hands of the Nazis, removed it from a Rome bank vault for safekeeping. The trophy spent the war stashed away in a shoe box under the bed of another soccer official.

The trophy survived the war only to disappear in 1966, while on display at a London stamp exhibition, preceding that year's World Cup finals. Fortunately, a dog named **Pickles** saved the day when he discovered the trophy under a garden hedge only a few days before the tournament began.

When Brazil won the World Cup for a record third time in 1950, the country was allowed to keep the trophy permanently. However, no sooner had the trophy gone on public display than it was stolen, never to be found again. Its replacement, designed by Italian sculptor **Silvio Gazamiga**, is the 15-inch-high gold trophy that's officially known as the FIFA World Cup. Each winning player receives a small replica of the famous trophy.

Players

The best soccer **shoes** are made of calf or kangaroo leather—the more lightweight, snug-fitting, and durable the better. Today's shoes have polyurethane or rubber soles with anywhere from six to 18 studs (or cleats), either molded directly or separately screwed into the sole. Long, thick studs provide good traction on wet, muddy fields; small, flat studs work well on artificial surfaces. Traditions die hard in soccer, so black continues to be the overwhelming color of choice for soccer shoes, but they now come in a rainbow of colors as well. Prices begin around $20 and quickly work their way up to $200 for the ultimate in stylish footwear.

Knee-length **socks**—secured above the calf muscle and below the knee with elastic or a gauze strip. Cost: $3 to $15 a pair.

Thin, lightweight **shinguards** are worn between the sock and the shin. Invented in England in 1874, they are the only protective padding worn by soccer players. Cost: $5 to $45.

Nylon **shorts,** with an elastic waistband or drawstring, are typically either the same color as the shirt or a contrasting color. A player's number appears at the bottom on the front. Cost: $10 to $35.

Tight-fitting, elastic **bicycle shorts** are often worn beneath the nylon shorts for added support and flexibility. Cost: $15 to $30.

Nylon **shirts** come in a variety of distinctive color schemes and styles (many international teams favor shoulder chevrons, for instance). The back of the shirt carries the name of the player and his or her number; the front often shows the player's number and sometimes (mainly for club teams) the name of a sponsoring firm or organization. Cost: $15 to $65.

Goalie

A goalie's **shirt** must be a different color from that of his or her teammates; initially, yellow was prescribed for international matches, but in 1956 **FIFA** ruled that any color could be worn. Cost: $15 to $65.

Sometimes goalies wear slightly longer **shorts** than their teammates (with special hip and quadriceps padding), or even long pants. Cost: $20 to $35.

Shoes and **socks** are identical to those of other teammates. Cost: Shoes, $20 to $200; Socks, $3 to $15.

A goalkeeper's most important piece of equipment is a sturdy, durable pair of **gloves** with special pimpled rubber gripping. Cost: $10 to $75.

The goalie's **cap** shades his or her eyes from the sun. Cost: $15 to $20.

Playing Field

The fields where early forms of soccer were played varied considerably. Pre-Columbian ball games resembling soccer took place in North and Central America on specially constructed stone courts about 50 feet long, shaped like the Roman numeral I. In the 13th century, the annual **Shrovetide Football Game** in Ashbourne, England, took place on a field two miles long intersected by several streams and bounded by two old watermills that served as goals. And in Renaissance Italy, the huge Piazza di Santa Croce in the center of Florence functioned as the field for an early forerunner of soccer called *calcio* played by the local aristocracy.

It wasn't until the 19th century that England's public schools (the equivalent of private schools in the United States) revolutionized soccer by confining their matches to a parcel of open ground. One of the early pioneers, Harrow School, which codified its rules as far back as 1830, had to play on the only available field nearby, which was no more than 150 yards long and a hundred yards wide. Other schools, including Cambridge University, quickly embraced these dimensions. Soccer fields the world over have essentially remained the same size ever since.

The Field Itself

In England, the **Football Association's** first organized set of laws in 1863 established a maximum field length of 200 yards and a maximum width of 100 yards, required **corner flags,** and called for two upright posts eight feet apart as a **goal.** Two years later, it adopted a rule allowing a tape to be stretched across the top of the posts, but a proper **crossbar** didn't appear until 1883, the same year that **touchlines** were added to all sides of the field (the word "touchline," which is still used to denote the sidelines, refers to touching down the ball out of bounds to score). Soon thereafter came the **center spot** and **center circle,** but not until the early 20th century were the **halfway line** and the present **goal area, penalty area,** and **penalty spot** instituted. The semicircular **penalty arc** didn't make its appearance until 1937.

The field dimensions used today came into being in 1897, although initially the Football Association decreed that international matches should be played on a slightly smaller field than domestic matches. **The Fédération Internationale de Football Association (FIFA)** now requires the field for international matches to be 120 yards by 80 yards maximum and 110 yards by 75 yards minimum. The rules state that the field must be rectangular.

A soccer field is considerably wider than a football field. In the early days of the **North American Soccer League,** when many teams were forced to play on football fields, this proved to be a problem, cramping play toward the middle of the field and depriving many non-American players of the amount of space they were used to.

Today, the biggest controversy with regard to the field focuses on what it's made of—grass or plastic.

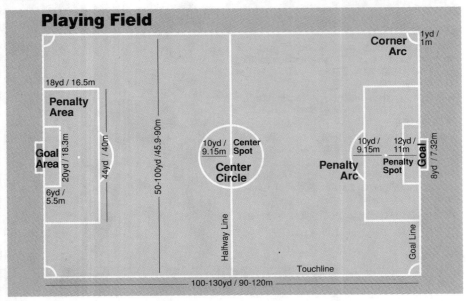

Playing Field

- Corner Arc — 1yd / 1m
- 18yd / 16.5m
- Penalty Area
- Goal Area
- 20yd / 18.3m
- 44yd / 40m
- 50-100yd / 45.9-90m
- 6yd / 5.5m
- 10yd / 9.15m — Center Spot
- Center Circle
- Halfway Line
- Penalty Arc
- 10yd / 9.15m
- 12yd / 11m — Penalty Spot
- Goal
- 8yd / 7.32m
- Goal Line
- Touchline
- 100-130yd / 90-120m

Soccer's founding fathers had always intended the sport to be played on grass, but then along came artificial turf. The debate began in 1966, when Real Madrid of Spain and West Ham United of England played an exhibition match at the Houston Astrodome on artificial grass. In 1976, FIFA allowed Syria and Iraq to play a World Cup qualifying match on an artificial surface in Riyadh, Saudi Arabia. Then, in the 1980s, Queens Park Rangers and Luton Town, both members of England's Football League, switched to plastic turf; but it provoked such an outcry from other clubs that they soon reverted to the real thing. Now FIFA has made it clear that for the World Cup finals, all matches must be played on the genuine green stuff.

The twin problems of size and playing surface reared up again when the United States was chosen to host the 1994 World Cup. Several of the stadiums selected have artificial fields used for football. In Giants Stadium, just outside New York, for example, not only did the artificial turf have to be covered by a layer of fresh green sod for the soccer matches, but several front-row seats had to be removed in order to widen the field to 73 yards—still a couple of yards short of the 75-yard minimum. But FIFA chose to accept these compromises, since it couldn't hold the World Cup finals in the United States without scheduling matches in the New York area.

For the 1994 World Cup, FIFA also relented on another previous taboo, permitting indoor matches at the Pontiac Silverdome, just outside of Detroit. Indoor play is now possible owing to agronomic advances—real grass can grow in a covered stadium under artificial light.

The Goal

The width of a soccer goal has remained eight feet ever since the dimensions were laid down in the landmark 1863 Football Association rules. But today's goal is much more sophisticated than the one conceived over a century ago. After the crossbar appeared in 1883, nets were then introduced in 1890-91, although to this day the official laws do not actually mandate their use or specify what materials they should be made of (hemp, jute, and nylon are the most common materials). However, the laws clearly stipulate that the goal posts and crossbars must be made of wood, metal, or another approved material; that they should be square, rectangular, round, half round, or elliptical in shape; and that their width and depth should not exceed five inches. Goal posts must be white, but no color is mentioned for the crossbar, so technically a duotone goal is possible.

The Field Markings

All the line markings on a soccer field must be of a uniform width, not exceeding five inches wide and

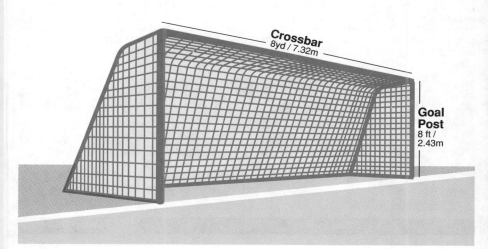

Crossbar
8yd / 7.32m

Goal Post
8 ft / 2.43m

Top Ten Soccer Books

The Encyclopedia of World Soccer by Richard Henshaw (New Republic Books, 1979). An incredibly detailed and fascinating look at soccer throughout the globe.

The Guinness Record of World Soccer by Guy Oliver (Guinness Publishing, 1992). A statistician's dream.

The Simplest Game by Paul Gardner (Collier, 1994). A wonderfully opinionated book by America's top soccer columnist.

NASL: A Complete Record of the North American Soccer League by Colin Jose (Breedon Books Sports, 1989). Essential reading for NASL junkies.

Only a Game? by Eamon Dunphy (Penguin, 1976) A revealing insider's view of British soccer in the early 1970s.

Champions of Europe by Brian Glanville (Guinness Publishing, 1991). One of soccer's most controversial journalists reviews the European club competitions.

The History of the World Cup by Brian Glanville (Faber & Faber, 1980). The definitive guide to the world's major soccer tournament.

Mordillo Football (Hutchinson, 1981). A hilarious collection by soccer's most celebrated cartoonist.

Soccer Skills and Tactics by Ken Jones & Pat Welton (Crown, 1976). An in-depth look at how to play the game, with wonderful illustrations.

Bryan Robsons' Soccer Skills (Sterling Publishing, 1987). The former England captain covers all the basics aided by excellent color photographs.

...and the Best in Soccer Journalism

Soccer America (Berling Publications, Berkeley, California, weekly). Since 1971, the bible for any American soccer fan.

World Soccer (IPC Magazines, London, monthly). Unbelievably comprehensive coverage of soccer in every corner of the world.

---

matching the width and depth of the goal posts, so that the inside and outside edges of both line up. These lines count as part of the field—if any part of a soccer ball is touching any part of a line, the ball is considered in play. Only when the whole ball crosses the line—either on the ground or in the air—is it ruled out of play. And for a goal to count, the entire ball must cross the goal line between the posts and under the crossbar.

A soccer field is not complete without four corner flagposts, although two additional halfway flagposts are optional. All these flagposts must be at least five feet high, so that they do not present a danger to players. In a much celebrated incident, the famous English referee **Jack Taylor** had to delay the start of the 1974 World Cup final in Munich when he realized local officials had forgotten all the flagposts.

Ball in Play   **Ball out of Play**

Soccer's popularity extends to the world's rich and famous. Here's a list of some prominent personalities, past and present, and their favorite teams:

Elton John   Watford (England)
John watched Watford during his boyhood, then bought the club and owned it for several years; he also was part owner of the Los Angeles Aztecs in the North American Soccer League.

Henry Kissinger   New York Cosmos
Kissinger played a key role in convincing FIFA to hold the 1994 World Cup Finals in the United States.

Madonna   Italy

The Pope   Poland

Omar Sharif   Egypt
Sharif once played for the Egyptian club National in a match against Pelé.

Rod Stewart   Scotland
The pop singer abandoned a pro soccer career at 19 to go into rock music; he founded the LA Exiles amateur team in 1985, and plays for them whenever his schedule allows.

Rules

Modern soccer as we know it was born on 26 October 1863, when officials from 11 fledgling English soccer clubs gathered at the Freemason's Tavern in London not only to form the world's first soccer association, but also to set about fashioning a set of universal rules to govern the playing of their fast-growing sport. The **Laws of the Game** were finally approved a few months later, but not before several members who favored what was called "the handling game" walked out in a huff and decided to form a breakaway sport that later became known as rugby (a forerunner of U.S. and Canadian football, as well as Australian rules football).

Although little of what was decided in 1863 remains in force today, it's still largely the British who determine the rules for the rest of the world. The English, Scottish, Welsh, and Irish associations, meeting in 1882 to update the laws, decided to give themselves the grand title of the **International Football Association Board.** When the **Fédération Internationale de Football Association (FIFA)** came into being as the world's governing body for soccer in 1904, the British had already established rule-making hegemony. Not until 1913 did the four British associations see fit to allow two FIFA representatives to join their regulatory body. Even today, the 20 members of the board—still responsible for reviewing and changing the laws annually—consist of four representatives from each of the four British associations, plus one representative each from four other FIFA member nations.

The Referee

In all soccer matches, final authority rests with a single official, the referee, who has the unenviable job of enforcing the rules, maintaining order among the players, checking the players' equipment, keeping score, and acting as timekeeper. As such, refereeing tends to be a hazardous profession likely to incur the wrath of players, coaches, spectators, and anyone else with a vested interest in the game. The 1976 World Cup qualifying match between Cameroon and Zaire is a perfect case in point. When the "impartial" Gambian referee awarded a penalty kick to Cameroon, he was attacked by Zaire's enraged goalkeeper, setting off a huge fight among all of the players, which quickly escalated into a spectator brawl. Paratroopers were sent in by helicopter to restore order, but not before two Cameroon fans had been killed.

In Pocket
Notebook/pencil
Coin
Stopwatch
Extra whistle
Extra pencil
Yellow card/Red card
Wristwatch

In gentler times, back in the mid-19th century, soccer matches were officiated in the same way as cricket—by two umpires (one supplied by each team) who were responsible for their respective halves of the field; the players "appealed" to them for a particular decision. A neutral referee was used in the England's **Football Association (F.A.) Cup** final of 1871 to help resolve disagreements with the umpires' decisions, but not until 20 years later were umpires finally consigned to the sidelines and an independent referee given full control on the field.

Referees started out as amateurs, and this is essentially the way things remain today. Only Brazil and Italy have full-time professional referees. Officials earn a pittance compared to the mega-salaries paid the players, coaches, and administrators. In the English League, for instance, referees receive a measly £100 per match, and even in Italy's Serie A championship, where players routinely receive six-figure salaries, referees earn no more than $30,000 a year.

The first referees donned black uniforms, a tradition that continues, although the rules merely stipulate that for international matches the official "shall wear a blazer or blouse the color of which is distinctive from the colors worn by the contesting teams."

Not only do international matches have to be refereed by officials from neutral countries, they must also be on a select list of specially approved referees. In 1993, more than a thousand officials were on this exclusive FIFA list, including seven from the United States.

The Linesmen

Linesmen appeared for the first time on a soccer field in 1891. Then, as now, their job was to assist referees by running up and down the touchlines and signaling when the ball went out of play, thereby indicating which team should receive corner kicks, goal kicks, or throw-ins. Since linesmen need to keep up with where the ball is in play, they are also usually in a good position to signal whether a player is offside or not (see this chapter, page 11). Furthermore, if linesmen see any infractions on the field that they believe the referee may have missed, they must signal to the official. But the referee can still overrule the linesmen at any time—usually because the official is in a better position to see what actually happened.

Linesmen wear the same black clothing as referees, but they are equipped with a brightly colored (usually red or yellow) flag on a short stick that they wave to draw the referee's attention.

The job of linesman is an intermediate step for anyone attempting to gain certification as a referee. For international matches, however, all linesmen are fully qualified referees who appear on the FIFA-approved list—and like referees, they must always come from a neutral country to ensure impartiality.

Fouls

In the early years of soccer, brute force often carried the day, but as the sport became more sophisticated and more organized, officials made an attempt to regulate violent conduct. The Football Association's 1863 laws stated: "Neither tripping nor hacking shall be allowed, and no player shall use his hands to hold or push his adversary." In ensuing years, this simple clause was expanded to produce a list of offenses, called fouls, that a referee could observe a player committing and punish by awarding a free kick to the opposing team. There are two kinds of free kicks: direct and indirect. With a **direct free kick,** a player can score a goal without anyone else having to touch the ball, while with an **indirect free kick,** at least one other player in addition to the kicker must touch the ball before it enters the net.

The most serious fouls, when committed intentionally, result in a direct free kick—or a **penalty kick** (an unimpeded shot by a player against the opposing goalkeeper) if the foul is committed by the offending player in his or her own penalty area.

Direct free kick fouls include:
Kicking an opponent (including an over-the-ball tackle).

Tripping an opponent (including a poorly executed tackle).

Jumping at an opponent (when the offending player makes no attempt to play the ball).

Charging an opponent in a violent or dangerous way, including charging a player from behind, unless he or she is guilty of obstruction. (Charging another player by leaning your shoulder against his or her shoulder (with arms and elbows tucked in) when the ball is within playing distance is permitted as a **fair charge.**)

(Striking an opponent (spitting at a player is considered striking, as is a goalkeeper's deliberately throwing the ball at an opponent).

Pushing an opponent.

Holding an opponent (including pulling a player's shirt).

Handling the ball intentionally with any part of the arm or hand (an exception is made for the goalkeeper in his or her own penalty area).

All other fouls are punished with an indirect free kick. The referee signals an indirect free kick by raising an arm above his or her head, so that players and fans can distinguish it from a direct free kick.

Indirect free kick fouls include:
Dangerous play, by high kicking a ball close to an opponent's head or attempting to kick a ball held by the opposing goalkeeper.

Making a fair charge on an opponent when the ball is not within playing distance.

Obstruction, by blocking or impeding (with one's body) an opponent's attempt to reach a ball that is not within playing distance.

Other Misconduct

Referees must also punish several lesser offenses by awarding an indirect free kick. These offenses include:

- making a fair charge on the opposing goalkeeper in the goal area when he or she isn't holding the ball (but a player can make a fair charge if the goalkeeper is obstructing an opponent);

- goalkeepers taking more than four steps while playing the ball with their hands, although they can take as many steps as needed if they play the ball with their feet (and after releasing the ball, goalkeepers cannot touch it again with their hands until another player has touched it);

- goalkeepers wasting time by holding the ball longer than necessary;

- goalkeepers using their hands within the penalty area to play a ball kicked to them by a teammate (they can, however, handle the ball if it's played to them with the head or the chest).

Cautions and Ejections

Professional soccer has grown increasingly competitive, with foul play and misconduct becoming steadily more persistent. As a result, referees can now give players who commit certain serious offenses an official warning, or caution; because the offending player's name must be entered in the referee's notebook, this has become known as "booking a player." For an even more serious offense, referees also have the option of ejecting a player. Once removed from the match, the player cannot reappear.

In the 1968 Olympics, FIFA experimented with referees holding up a yellow card to indicate a caution and a red card to show an ejection. This all-too-familiar practice has been used worldwide ever since. If a player is given a yellow card caution and then commits another yellow card offense, he or she automatically receives a red card ejection. Referees must report any cautions and ejections in a particular match to the governing body responsible for the match; that governing body can then take disciplinary action against the players involved, usually in the form of suspensions and/or fines.

Receiving a red card or two yellows in an international match automatically earns a player a suspension of at least one game, and the more serious the offense, the longer the suspension. Different governing bodies dole out different degrees of punishment. For example, if a player strikes an official in a match governed by U.S. Soccer, he or she will automatically be suspended for one year.

Yellow Card Offenses

Yellow card offenses, are punishable by awarding a free kick (direct or indirect, depending upon the nature of the offense) to the other team. They are:

Entering or reentering the field without being signaled to do so by the referee.

Expressing verbal or any other kind of dissent to a decision by the referee or linesmen (such as arguing with a referee or kicking the ball away in anger).

Persistently breaking soccer's official laws, such as repeatedly pushing, holding, or tripping.

Engaging in what the laws euphemistically describe as "ungentlemanly conduct," such as distracting an opponent by shouting, wasting time, or feigning injury.

Red Card Offenses

Most serious of all are **red card offenses,** for which a player must be ejected and a free kick (direct or indirect, depending upon the nature of the offense) awarded to the other team. They are:

Being involved in excessive and violent play, including spitting at an opponent.

Denying an opponent a clear goal-scoring opportunity by committing any of the direct free kick offenses listed above—this is known as committing a **professional foul.**

Using foul or abusive language.

Persisting in misconduct after already having received a caution.

The laws also explicitly state that any misconduct shown to the referee, even if it occurs off the field, should be dealt with as if it happened during a match. There have even been cases in which players were cautioned or ejected before or after a match—in a parking lot, outside a dressing room, and on the sidelines.

Offside

If it weren't for the offside rule, soccer's claim that it is the world's simplest sport would be perfectly believable. Offside, though it is far and away the most complex rule, is a necessary evil. Without it soccer would probably degenerate into a contest devoid of skill between hordes of players gathered around each goal trying either to score at close range or kick the ball to the other end of the field.

This sorry possibility wasn't lost on soccer's pioneers. As early as 1848, the proponents of the Cambridge University rules only allowed a player to receive a forward pass if more than three opponents were between him or her and the goal line. The English Football Association embraced this early form of offside in 1866, then tinkered with various minor changes before taking the radical step in 1925 of reducing the number of opponents from three to two. The only other significant change occurred in 1990, with the concession that a player level with one or both opponents would no longer be considered offside.

Simply stated, the laws consider a player offside if he or she is nearer an opponent's goal line than the ball at the moment the ball is last played, unless:

1. The player is on his or her own half of the field.

2. There are two opponents nearer their own goal line than the player.

3. The ball was last touched by an opponent or was last played by the player.

4. The player receives the ball from a goal kick, corner kick, throw-in, or drop ball.

Offside, though, is subjective. If, in the opinion of the referee, a player is in an offside position but not interfering with play (or an opponent) or trying to gain an advantage, that player is not offside.

When a referee calls a player offside, an indirect free kick is awarded to the other team from the point where the player is caught offside.

If offside still seems confusing, consider the illustrations on the following pages.

Defending teams sometimes attempt to catch their opponents offside by using the offside trap. To be executed perfectly, all defenders (other than the goalkeeper) must remain just behind any opposing attacking players, and then a split second before another opponent plays the ball forward, they must move in front of the players before they have a chance to react. This procedure relies on the linesmen and/or referee being particularly observant.

The Advantage Rule

The best soccer matches invariably turn out to be those where the role of the referee is hardly noticed. The less intervention needed from a referee, the better. Soccer even has a law that attempts to turn this into reality. In 1903, the advantage rule was introduced, allowing a referee to choose not to stop a match to penalize a player for an offense if he or she feels that doing so might actually benefit the offending team.

The following is a good example of how a referee might apply the advantage rule: while sprinting toward the goal with only one opponent and the

B is offside because at the moment A plays the ball to him, he is in front of the ball and there are not two opponents nearer the goal line (only goalkeeper X is nearer the goal line).

Offside

B is not offside because at the moment A plays the ball to him, there are two opponents (goalkeeper X and defender Y) nearer the goal line; in this case, the 1990 rule change applies, since B is level with Y and, therefore, Y is considered nearer the goal line.

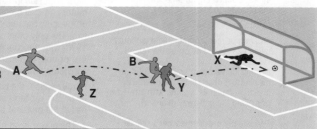

Not Offside

B is offside, although when he runs back to receive the pass from A, he is not offside (goalkeeper X and defenders Y and Z are nearer the goal line). The rule is determined by A's position when the ball was played—and at that moment A was offside (only goalkeeper X was nearer the goal line).

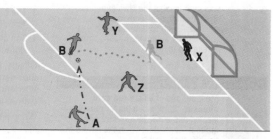

Offside

A is not offside because when he dribbles through the opposing defense and shoots, the ball hits the crossbar and A scores off the rebound; although A is in an offside position, this doesn't apply because he himself last played the ball.

Not Offside

A is not offside because when he dribbles through the opposing defense and shoots, goalkeeper X deflects the ball to B, who scores; although A is in an offside position, this doesn't apply because the ball was last touched by an opponent, goalkeeper X.

Not Offside

B is offside because at the moment A kicks the ball, there are not two opponents nearer the goal line and he is clearly interfering with play by obstructing goalkeeper X.

Offside

B is not offside because at the moment A kicks the ball—although there are not two opponents nearer the goal line, he is clearly not involved in the action and therefore not interfering with play.

Not Offside

goalkeeper to beat in order to have a clear shot at the goal, a player is illegally tackled by the opponent or the goalie. Ordinarily, the referee would blow his or her whistle, call the foul, and give the attacking team a direct free kick. But this would allow the offending team to bring back all its players, giving them a good chance to successfully deal with the free kick. However, if the player, despite the severity of the foul, is somehow able to stumble on toward the goal, the referee can invoke the advantage rule and allow the player to recover and continue his or her attacking run. It's actually much more likely that the player will score from this opportunity than from the direct free kick. As soon as the ball is dead, the referee still has the option of dealing with the errant defender by cautioning or ejecting him or her if such punishment is appropriate.

A good referee knows how to use the advantage rule to keep a match moving—an important consideration now that a foul is committed every three minutes in major matches such as the World Cup finals.

Timekeeping

In soccer, the referee is the official timekeeper, and since he or she uses his or her wristwatch or a stopwatch, nobody else in the stadium knows precisely how much time is left in a match at a particular moment. No scoreboard clock or other stadium mechanism displays the official time.

All professional matches are split into two 45-minute halves, with an interval between them that must last a minimum of five minutes, but usually takes somewhere between 10 and 15 minutes. At the referee's discretion, he or she can add on time lost for such things as making substitutions, treating seriously injured players, and time-wasting, which means that a typical half usually runs a minute or two longer than the statutory 45 minutes. But if the referee awards a penalty kick just seconds before

the expiration of either half, he or she must allow whatever time necessary for the kick.

In certain World Cup matches and other international competitions, a tie at the end of regulation play needs to be resolved. Usually a 30-minute overtime (split into two 15-minute halves) is played, although in the future many matches will be decided by sudden death overtime, in which the first team that scores automatically wins. If this still doesn't settle matters, either the match will be replayed in its 90-minute entirety at another time or a penalty kick "shootout" will be held, with both teams nominating five players who in turn each take a penalty kick against the opposing goalkeeper. If the scores remain even at the end of the fifth round, each team continues taking alternate penalty kicks until a winner is determined. Nobody seems to like it when important matches are settled this way—both semi-finals in the 1990 World Cup were decided by a penalty kick shootout—but until someone comes up with a better alternative, it remains a fact of soccer life.

In certain extreme cases, a referee may have to suspend a match—perhaps because of severe weather, such as heavy lightning, blinding snow, or impenetrable fog, or sometimes due to crowd disturbances, stadium accidents, and natural disasters.

Soccer can exert a powerful influence on the populace. Ecuadorans, for instance, were galvanized by their country's inspired performance during the 1993 Copa America, when the team swept every obstacle before them to reach the semi-final against Mexico. On the morning of the vital match, Ecuadorans were asked to select the biggest problem facing their country. Twenty-six percent thought it was "how to lower inflation," 22 percent selected "how to raise salaries," and 52 percent chose "how to beat Mexico."

Players

Soccer teams have been composed of 11 players since the first official set of laws appeared in the middle of the 19th century, a far cry from the days in medieval England when the inhabitants of an entire village teamed up to play soccer against everyone in a neighboring community. The first "organized" matches in the 1800s bore little resemblance to those of today. Initially, forward passing was prohibited, so the only way to make any progress was to dribble the ball from one foot to the other. Most teams used a forward line of at least seven or eight attackers—all dribbling specialists—with a couple of players just behind them for support. Only one lone defender was stationed at the back to stop all these dribblers, and even the goalkeeper could roam the field at will, handling the ball whenever necessary. A properly organized defense didn't make its first appearance until the 1880s, and midfielders are very much a 20th-century phenomenon.

Ironically, many of today's teams use more midfielders than either defensive or attacking players. In fact, a recent survey shows that an average midfielder runs about seven miles a game, compared to strikers and fullbacks who run five miles, central defenders four miles, and goalkeepers two-and-a-half miles.

Goalkeeper

The only player on the field allowed to use his or her hands is the goalkeeper (aside from one exception, when players take **throw-ins**—see chapter 6, page 19), making this soccer's most specialized job. When the position was officially recognized by England's revised Football Association laws in 1870, goalkeepers could handle the ball anywhere in their defensive half of the field. Only in 1912 were they restricted to using their hands solely within their own penalty area.

Goalkeepers tend to be acrobatic, courageous types with good hand-eye coordination. Their prime job, of course, is to defend their 192-square-yard home. It tends to be a high stress occupation, since it only takes one mistake by a goalkeeper to affect the outcome of a match. And pressure on goalkeepers has increased in recent years with the advent of penalty kick shootouts to resolve tied matches.

Unlike their teammates, goalkeepers face one direction during a match, and since they can appreciate what's happening on the field as a whole, they are usually good at communicating with the defenders in front of them and anticipating the opposition's moves.

Apart from knowing when to catch, punch, or deflect the ball, goalkeepers must have a good sense of when to remain on their goal line and when to leave it. Some goalkeepers advance so far forward that they almost function as a second stopper in the defensive line, but this can be risky.

Frequently overlooked is the offensive role of a goalkeeper: a goalie can set a swift attack in motion by throwing the ball to a teammate or kicking it downfield to a well-placed striker. A few goalkeepers have even been known to score a goal or two, mainly from the penalty spot.

Defenders

Defenders once were expected to prevent the opposition from scoring and nothing else. But recently, they have taken on a more creative, positive

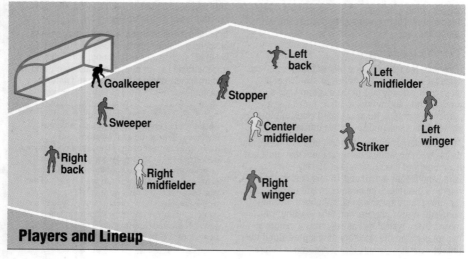

Players and Lineup

role. Whenever possible, they move forward to assist the midfielders and forwards, which requires strong **tackling** skills (the ability to take the ball away from an opponent), the ability to head the ball well and accelerate quickly, and solid all-around skills.

Most teams employ four defenders strung across the back of the field, hence the use of general terms such as **backs** or **back four.** Three of these players usually mark (guard) the opposing team's forwards, with the fourth working in a freelance capacity, assisting wherever necessary. Some teams use **zone defense,** also known as a **zone marking system,** in which each of the four defenders is responsible for a specific part of the field, covering any opponent who enters that particular area.

Fullbacks

The left and right fullbacks (also called **left** and **right backs)** operate on the flanks, guarding whoever attacks down the side; sometimes the attacker is a winger, but usually it's a midfielder. The fullback's objective is to keep an opponent as close to the touchline as possible, preventing him or her from cutting inside along the goal line. One of the best duels in soccer is between a speedy winger with great dribbling skills and a tenacious fullback with equally outstanding tackling skills. Fullbacks are also expected to look for opportunities to attack, by overlapping, or surging forward, down the flank. For this type of maneuver, the capacity to cross the ball (kick the ball into the air toward the penalty area from near the touchline) is essential.

Stopper

Most teams have two central defenders, also called **center backs,** who operate in the two middle defense positions. When a team plays zone defense, both center backs have the same role, but for the more commonly used **man-to-man marking system,** teams normally divide the responsibilities between a stopper and a **sweeper.** The former usually marks the opponents' most dangerous striker. A top-notch stopper must have good heading and tackling skills. Since the stopper works in the busiest part of the field—the middle—he or she is rarely able to move forward. But because most stoppers are tall and strong and therefore capable of heading the ball well, they often go into the opposing penalty area for important set plays, such as **corner kicks** and **free kicks** (see chapter 6, pages 19-20).

Sweeper

This position was introduced in the 1960s by the Italians, who are famous for their *catenaccio* (literally "great chain") defense. The sweeper (or *libero,* meaning "free one") was initially intended as a roaming last line of defense to deal with, or

Soccer players are always on the move. The accomplished Dutch midfielder Johan Neeskens once lost 12 pounds in the course of a North American Soccer League match he played for the New York Cosmos.

"sweep up," any opponents' attacks that managed to get past the other three defenders. But lately, the position has acquired even more freedom, allowing sweepers to overlap down the middle of the field when space opens up in front of them. A good sweeper must be expert at tackling, have an outstanding ability for reading and interpreting plays, and possess strong running and excellent passing skills.

Midfielders

Originally known as halfbacks, midfielders operate across the central portion of the field, providing a vital link between defenders and forwards. On receiving the ball from defenders, they move it downfield and set it up for the forwards. As soccer has grown more defensive—an ever-increasing number of forwards are taking position farther back on the field to act as midfielders—dominance over the midfield area has gained importance.

Today, most teams have anywhere from three to five midfielders. At least one or two of them are **defensive midfielders,** operating in front of the defenders, with the primary task of getting the ball and feeding it to their colleagues, the **attacking midfielders.** Sometimes a defensive midfielder will be assigned to guard a particularly dangerous attacking midfielder on the other team. But more often than not, he or she is expected to cover vast areas of the field, energetically tackling players and intercepting the ball whenever possible. Defensive midfielders should also have good short-range passing skills and a keen eye for situations that they can turn to their team's advantage.

In contrast, attacking midfielders are more concerned with creating scoring opportunities for their attacking teammates or actually moving forward and scoring goals themselves. They need good ball control, superb passing skills, fine shooting ability, and acumen for keeping up with and reading plays.

The distinction between defensive and attacking midfielders is blurring as more and more players are expected to perform both functions equally well. Many teams now line up with left and right midfielders on the flanks and several midfielders patrolling the center.

Forwards

No more glamorous position exists in soccer than that of forward: these players score most of the goals and therefore hog most of the limelight. But with this high visibility comes a great deal of pressure, especially since teams have gradually reduced the number of forwards in their lineups, which has caused the number of goals to steadily decline. In the golden days of attacking soccer (it has since evolved into a far more defensive game), a typical forward line featured five players—two outside forwards (called **wingers**), a **center forward,** and **two inside forwards**—but now most teams play with no more than three forwards—two central attackers (known as **strikers**) and perhaps one winger.

Strikers

When receiving passes from midfielders and attacking defenders, strikers must be able to bring the ball quickly under control, take it past an opponent, and, most important of all, put it into the net. Speed, timing, and agility are all essential attributes for this position. Strikers often have to endure remorseless punishment from opposing defenders and be prepared to make enormous physical efforts in order to score goals. A lone striker, in the classic center forward tradition, must be extremely powerful at both heading and playing the ball on the ground.

Wingers

Many teams have stopped using wingers altogether, employing just one or two strikers up front, but a few have managed to thrive. These entertaining players operate close to the touchline, relying on their speed and dribbling ability to get them behind the opposing defense, where they can either cross the ball into the middle for one of the strikers or continue dribbling along the goal line. Always looking for open space, wingers must also be ready to take on opponents at any time and shoot, often from an oblique angle, with either foot.

Tactical Formations

Tactics do not play nearly as important a role in soccer as they do in other stop-and-start sports such as football, baseball, and basketball. Instead, soccer is an intuitive, fluid game. Only in set plays, such as corners and free kicks, can particular maneuvers be planned in advance.

By far the biggest tactical concern over the years has been balancing offense and defense. For some 30 years, from the 1930s until the 1960s, many countries adopted the classic **W-M formation,** so-called because the positions of the players form these letters on the field. In this formation, comprised of five defenders and five forwards, the

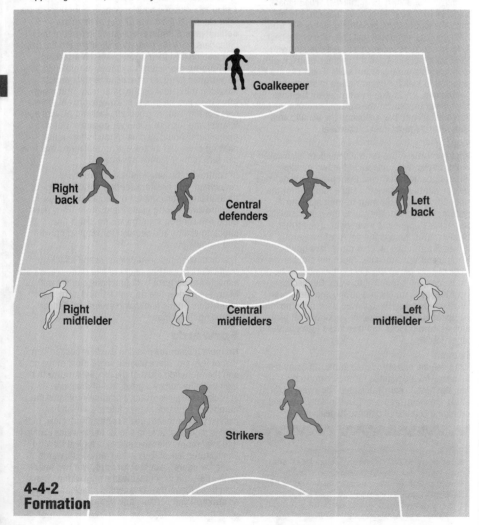

Goalkeeper

Right back

Central defenders

Left back

Right midfielder

Central midfielders

Left midfielder

Strikers

4-4-2 Formation

two halfbacks pushed a little ahead of the defense and the two inside forwards were somewhat withdrawn from the other attackers.

The W-M formation disappeared in the 1960s when soccer entered a new defensive era spearheaded by the Italians, who began using a ruthless five-defender *catenaccio* system, and the English, whose "wingless wonders" won the 1966 World Cup with just two strikers. By the 1970s, a new **4-3-3 formation** had evolved, still widely used today, with four defenders (two outside backs, a stopper, and a sweeper), three midfielders, and three forwards (usually two strikers and a left or right winger).

Soccer has been played cautiously in recent years. With an increasing emphasis on midfield dominance, the **4-4-2 formation** (see page 16) has come into vogue. In this formation, four defenders are deployed, but the midfield gains one player at the expense of the forward line. Conventional wingers are eliminated, although fullbacks and midfielders can still perform some of their functions. Of the two central midfielders, one is normally defensive and the other attacks.

The present trend in formations is still toward packing the midfield. Some teams have even pulled one of the two remaining forwards (in the 4-4-2 formation) back into the midfield, leaving a single striker. Yet many players who might appear restricted to one particular position, in fact, play multiple positions. For instance, a left midfielder may spend much of his or her time in an attacking role, functioning almost as a left winger, before switching to a more conventional midfield defensive stance to help his or her team gain possession of the ball. Or this same midfielder may move back into a defensive position to help protect his or her team's narrow lead in the latter stages of a match. A player's capacity to assume all three roles (defense, midfield, offense) is part of the "total soccer" concept pioneered by the Dutch in the 1974 and 1978 World Cup finals.

Substitutions

One of the main reasons soccer has not assumed the tactical complexity of football or baseball is that it has never allowed mass or unlimited substitutions. Up until 1932, a player could not be replaced, even if he or she was injured. International matches after that date allowed for a single substitution in the case of an injury, providing both teams agreed to it. Then in 1967, FIFA sanctioned the use of two substitutions for injury or tactical reasons in international competition. In club matches in most parts of the world now, no more than five subsitutions can take place, still fewer than the five substitutions and unlimited re-substitutions allowed in U.S. collegiate soccer.

Rigid rules also govern how a substitution occurs in soccer. The referee must be informed in advance—the team usually displays a large panel with the number of the player it wants to replace and has the substitute waiting at the halfway line. The substitute can only enter the field when play has stopped and after the player he or she is replacing has left. Any player may change places with the goalkeeper, but the exchange of jerseys must wait until the referee has been advised during a pause in play.

For Love...And Money

The world's most expensive soccer player is Gianluigi Lentini, who in 1992 was transferred from Torino to Italian Serie A rival AC Milan for a record $21 million. The amount of money one team pays another team when a player is traded is known in soccer as a transfer fee. Before fees became so astronomical, a player would personally receive a percentage (often about 5 percent) of the transfer fee when he was traded. But now the size and extent of players' contracts, plus lucrative bonus provisions, have become far more significant factors. For instance, the Lentini transaction also included a four-year contract that paid the Italian star $1.2 million a year.

No transfer fee was involved when Pelé came out of retirement in 1975 to play for the New York Cosmos, but the contract he signed was reportedly somewhere between $3.5 million and $4.5 million, the largest amount ever paid to a soccer player.

Here's a brief look at how transfer fees have escalated over the years:

Year	Player	Teams	Fee
1892	Willie Groves	West Bromwich Albion to Aston Villa (England)	£100
1905	Alf Common	Sunderland to Middlesbrough (England)	£1,000
1928	David Jack	Bolton Wanderers to Arsenal (England)	£10,800
1954	Juan Schiaffino	Peñarol (Uruguay) to AC Milan (Italy)	$200,000
1968	Pietro Anastasi	Varese to Juventus (Italy)	$1.2 million
1973	Johan Cruyff	Ajax (Holland) to Barcelona (Spain)	$2.4 million
1977	Franz Beckenbauer	Bayern München (Germany) to N.Y. Cosmos (USA)	$2.5 million
1982	Diego Maradona	Boca Júniors (Argentina) to Barcelona (Spain)	$7.7 million
1984	Diego Maradona	Barcelona (Spain) to Napoli (Italy)	$11.1 million
1990	Robert Baggio	Fiorentina to Juventus (Italy)	$13 million
1992	Jean-Pierre Papin	Marseilles (France) to AC Milan (Italy)	$16 million
1992	Gianluigi Lentini	Torino to AC Milan (Italy)	$21 million

Plays

For a sport as relatively unprogrammed as soccer, the only predictable elements are **set plays** or set-piece plays that can be practiced and rehearsed in advance. Almost half of all goals scored in soccer result from **throw-ins, corner kicks, free kicks**, and **penalty kicks**. These pre-established plays have decided many an important match. Of course, not all of the plays in soccer can have such momentous impact. But even the humble **kick-off**, **goal kick**, and **drop ball** each have their appropriate place.

Although variety in set plays can work to a team's advantage in that they can catch the other team's players off guard or keep them guessing, sometimes the more direct and simple set plays are the most effective.

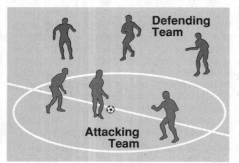

Defending Team

Attacking Team

Kick-off

Soccer matches have started with a kick-off at least as far back as the 1830s, when this play was first prescribed in England's **Harrow School Rules.** Just before the start of a match, the two rival captains meet in the center circle, shake hands, and sometimes exchange pennants and other team memorabilia. The referee usually handles the coin toss, with the visiting team captain calling heads or tails. The winning captain can either decide to take the kick-off or choose which half of the field to defend for the first 45 minutes.

The ball is then placed on the center spot. Each team's players must line up in their own half. Players on the team kicking off can be as close to the ball as they like, but all members of the opposing team must remain at least 10 yards away (i.e., outside the center circle) until the ball is kicked. As soon as the referee blows his or her whistle, the player kicking off must kick the ball forward into his or her opponents' half so that it travels at least the distance of its own circumference. When this happens play is officially underway, but the player kicking off is not allowed to touch the ball again until it has been played by another player.

Most kick-offs begin with a striker pushing the ball slightly ahead to a fellow striker or winger, who then passes it back to a midfielder to set up the first play of the match. Although a goal cannot be scored directly from a kick-off, a few have been scored one or two touches after a kick-off. Still, this is an extremely rare occurrence.

The opposing team gets to kick off to begin the second half. Every time a goal is scored, play restarts with a kick-off taken by the team that gave up the goal. Kick-offs also start each half of an overtime period.

Out of Play

When the ball leaves the field—except for when a goal is scored—there are three different ways of putting it back into play, depending upon which line it crossed and which player last touched it.

1

Throw-in to A

A

B

Throw-in to B

B

A

A ball sent across the touchline by either team results in a **throw-in** to the team that did not touch the ball last.

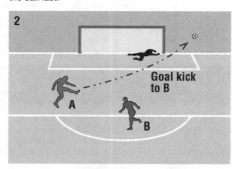

2

Goal kick to B

A

B

A ball sent across the goal line by the attacking team results in a **goal kick** for the defending team.

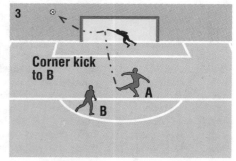

3

Corner kick to B

A

B

A ball sent across the goal line by the defending team results in a **corner kick** for the attacking team.

Throw-in

A team must take a throw-in as close as possible to the point where the ball went out of play. The player who throws the ball has to face the field, hold the ball with both hands, and have both feet on or behind the touchline. Part of each foot must remain on the ground, and the player must throw from behind the head and over it. Once the player has thrown the ball, he or she can't play it until another player has done so. If any of these infractions occur, the other team is awarded a throw-in from the same point.

The player closest to where the ball went out of play usually takes the throw-in. That person normally throws it to a teammate a short distance away. But if a team is near the opponent's goal, it may decide to have a player who specializes in taking throw-ins use a running start to throw the ball a long way into the penalty or goal area, aiming for a specific player. A few players even take a running start and do a forward somersault before releasing the ball to help them gain greater height and distance. Otherwise, the general rule of thumb for executing throw-ins is to look for an unguarded player (or one who can run into open space), preferably throw the ball in the direction of the opponent's goal, and make the ball as easy as possible to bring under control (ideally by throwing it directly to the teammate's feet).

Many goals result from well-executed throw-ins, especially those of the running long-distance variety, although the laws don't permit anyone to score directly from a throw-in.

The first player ever to score from a penalty kick was actually an American by the name of Jeffrey, who achieved the feat while playing for a combined U.S.-Canadian team against Linfield Football Club in Belfast, Northern Ireland in 1891.

Goal Kick

For a goal kick, the ball can be placed anywhere in the goal area on the side where the ball went out of play. Any player on the defending team may take this kick, which must clear the penalty area before another player on either team can touch it. Every player except the goal kicker must remain outside the penalty area until the ball is officially in play. Whoever takes the kick can't touch the ball again until another player has touched it. Failure to observe any of these rules results in the kick being retaken.

Most goal kicks used to be booted downfield by the goalkeeper, but, because this doesn't guarantee which team will take over the ball, it has now become more common for a goalkeeper or a fellow defender to kick the ball just outside the penalty area to a teammate, thus retaining possession and enabling teammates to start an attack. However, on a short kick it's crucial that the ball be passed to a clearly open player, since if an opponent gets hold of the ball, he or she will probably be in an excellent position to score. Although a team can't score directly from a goal kick, if it is desperate for goals, it will likely use these kicks to get the ball into its opponents' penalty area as quickly as possible.

Corner Kick

On a corner kick, the ball must be placed completely within the corner arc on the side where the ball went out of play. All opposing players have to remain 10 yards away until the designated player takes the kick. As with kick-offs, throw-ins, and goal kicks, once a player takes a corner kick, he or she cannot touch the ball again until another player does so, but unlike all these other set plays, a goal can be scored directly from a corner kick.

Most corner kicks are crossed into the penalty area, although sometimes, to catch the opponents off guard or to counteract windy conditions, the kicker will try a **short corner,** passing the ball along the ground to a nearby player to guarantee that the attacking team keeps the ball. But a team's best chance of scoring comes from a corner kick driven directly into the penalty area. Many players specialize in taking corner kicks. The secret is to cross the ball high enough for a teammate to head it toward the goal while also keeping it out of the opposing goalkeeper's reach.

Goal Kick

Corner Kick Outswinger

Of the two main kinds of corner kicks, the **outswinger** is the more popular. The corner kicker curves the ball away from the goal but toward the heads of his or her teammates, most of whom are stationed between the edges of the penalty and goal areas. The defending goalkeeper has an important but difficult choice to make: either to stay on his or her line, where it may be difficult to react to a powerfully driven header, or to come out and deal with the cross. But the defending goalkeeper must be sure to catch or parry it; otherwise, one of his or her teammates must deal with the ball.

Corner Kick Inswinger

For the second kind of corner kick, the **inswinger**, the kicker usually bends the ball in toward the near post (the closest goal post to the kicker), where a teammate can head it with a back header or flicked header (see page 30) across the goal. Again, the defending goalkeeper must either stay on the line and react to the consequences or move aggressively toward the ball, providing he or she isn't blocked in by opposing players.

For a team to defend itself well against corner kicks, it must have a confident, commanding goalkeeper and must concentrate on making sure all opponents in the penalty area are well marked, especially those who have good heading skills. Normally, one defender stands just inside the goal beside the near post and another in the same position beside the far post.

Free Kick

A free kick is awarded to a team when a foul or another kind of offense is committed by one of its opponents (see Chapter 4, page 10). The referee blows the whistle to stop play, and the ball is placed wherever the foul or offense took place. All the players on the opposing team must remain at least 10 yards away until the kick is taken, and the ball has to travel the distance of its circumference before play can officially restart. If a free kick is awarded inside the kicker's own penalty area, the opposing players must stay outside the area and the ball cannot be played until it clears the area. This means the goalkeeper can't receive the ball unless he or she leaves the penalty area and plays it with the feet, a risky move.

Free kicks come in two forms: **direct** and **indirect**. As the name implies, a direct free kick allows a player to score a goal without anyone else having to touch the ball. But to score from an indirect free kick, at least one other player (in addition to the kicker) must touch the ball before it enters the net. On an indirect free kick awarded less than 10 yards from the goal line, members of the defending team are allowed to stand on the goal line.

Most direct free kicks are fairly inconsequential until they occur within 40 yards or so of the goal. This is the point at which many players can shoot at the goal with some accuracy. To guard against such an occurrence, the penalized team usually erects a defensive wall made up of anywhere from two to six players standing close together. The goalkeeper must decide where the wall should be positioned so that he or she isn't screened during the free kick. But even these countermeasures will not stop a skillful kicker who can curve the ball around the wall or chip it over the top of the wall and make it dip under the crossbar. Another attacking ploy is to insert a player in the wall and have that person move aside just before the ball is kicked, thereby creating a gap that the kicker can exploit. Other offensive tactics include confusing the defending team by having two players ready to take the kick, one of whom fakes a shot, leaving the other to shoot at goal, or having one player look as if he is going to shoot but instead pass the ball to another player, who shoots from a completely different angle.

Similar tactics can be used on indirect free kicks. Otherwise most of these kicks are either crosses lofted into the penalty area aimed at teammates with good heading ability or short passes to teammates who can set another scoring opportunity in motion. A quickly taken kick can often reap dividends.

An attacking team has a big advantage at free kicks, but stringent man-to-man marking and quick reactions can still save the day for defending teams.

Penalty Kick

Any direct free kick violation committed by a player within his or her own penalty area results in an automatic penalty kick. The ball is placed on the penalty spot and any player from the team that has been fouled can take an unimpeded shot against the opposing goalkeeper. But as soon as the kicker

Free Kick

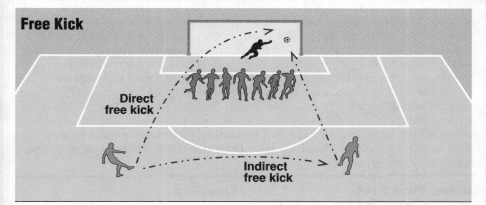

strikes the ball, he or she can't kick it again until another player has touched it. All other players have to stay out of the penalty area and be 10 yards from the ball—which means they must also remain outside the semicircular penalty arc—until the kick is taken. Meanwhile, the goalkeeper must keep both feet on the goal line and not move until the ball is hit. If the defending team violates any of these rules and the penalty kick has not resulted in a goal being scored, the kick must be retaken. If, however, the attacking team breaks any of these rules and a goal is scored, the kick must also be retaken.

In this classic confrontation between goalkeeper and penalty kicker, one would expect the kicker to always prevail. But in reality, only four out of every five penalties actually result in a goal. The goalie has a psychological advantage, since nobody expects a goalkeeper to be able to save a penalty kick, which relieves the pressure, but everybody believes the kicker will score, which puts pressure on him or her. Most teams appoint at least one specialist penalty taker, although with the increasing prevalence of penalty kick shootouts, more and more players are practicing this art.

The best place for the kicker to aim is the upper or lower corner of the goal, as far out of the goal-keeper's reach as possible. Most penalty takers decide beforehand which side of the goalkeeper to put the ball, to avoid any last-minute indecision or

hesitation. The more confident the kick, the better. All a goalkeeper can do is try and spoil the kicker's concentration or make an educated guess about which direction to dive, perhaps by determining a pattern from the kicker's past history of taking penalties. All other players must be lined up around the penalty area and arc, ready to react if the goalkeeper somehow parries the ball or if it bounces off the bar or post.

Drop Ball

Soccer's variation of basketball's jump ball or hockey's face-off is a drop ball, usually called by the referee when he or she has to interrupt a match for one of three reasons: because of an injury, when it is difficult to determine which team put the ball out of bounds, or when play has to be restarted after a substitute enters the field without the referee's permission. At the point where the incident occurred, the referee brings together one player from each team, has them stand face-to-face, then drops the ball between them. As soon as it hits the ground, the ball can be played. Drop balls are by far the rarest set play in soccer.

What Americans call an exhibition match is known as a *friendly* match in Britain, *match amical* in France, and *amichevole* in Italy.

Penalty Kick

Skills

"People are always kicking, old or young," says **Sepp Blatter**, Chief Executive Officer and General Secretary of FIFA, soccer's international governing body. "Even an unborn child is kicking." Perhaps this fact of nature helps explain soccer's worldwide popularity. Called football in just about every country in the world except the United States, Canada, and Australia, soccer is primarily played with the feet, which sets it apart from most of the other major sports, where the hands predominate. However, soccer's apparent simplicity is deceptive. Using the feet—and occasionally the head—to propel a ball up and down a large field looks relatively easy. But as this chapter—a short "soccer clinic"—shows, the sport actually involves an amazingly varied and diverse combination of skills. Learning and perfecting them takes a great deal of patience and practice. Once they have been mastered, the full beauty of the sport becomes apparent.

Using Your Feet

Although the tendency for most newcomers to soccer is to kick the ball with their toes, this is almost the only part of the foot that shouldn't be used. Not only is it tough on the toenails, but kicking with the toes makes it virtually impossible to control the ball properly. The parts of the foot that should be used are:

Inside The relatively large, flat area on the inside of the foot between the big toe and the ankle is used mainly for **passing** (because it ensures the greatest accuracy) and **trapping**.

Instep The small, flat surface on the side of the foot just under the arch is used mainly for long-distance passing and for shooting because the foot can extend for a good follow-through.

Top The curved area on the foot near the top of the shoe laces is used mainly for shooting because it offers the most power.

Outside The rounded area on the outside of the foot between the little toe and the ankle is used mainly for passing and shooting because it makes the ball curve.

Heel The rounded area on the back of the foot, occasionally used for passing.

Sole The flat bottom of the foot, occasionally used for trapping.

Trapping

The most basic skill in soccer is bringing the ball under control, which is called trapping. Yet this is also the skill most frequently overlooked. Unless you can trap the ball properly, you'll never be able to pass, shoot, dribble, or head it. The keys to good trapping are:

1. Keeping your eyes on the ball throughout play.
2. Moving quickly to and anticipating where to best make the trap.
3. Getting your body behind the ball in case it bounces badly or the particular trap you use doesn't work.
4. Deciding what part of your body to use for trapping the ball.
5. Cushioning the impact of the ball by relaxing the part of your body that traps the ball or actually pulling back a little if the ball is traveling fast; otherwise the ball is likely to ricochet.
6. Observing what's happening around you and on the rest of the field so that you can decide what to do with the ball once you have it under control.

Foot Trap

The easiest—and most common—way of bringing a ball under control is by trapping it on the ground with the inside part of the foot. As the ball comes toward you, turn your trapping foot to the side with the toes pointed outward and put it slightly behind your other foot. Bend your knees a little and lift your trapping foot sufficiently off the ground so that it's at approximately the same height as the center of the ball. Use the inside of your foot to absorb the impact of the ball and bring it under control. The technique is much the same when trapping an aerial

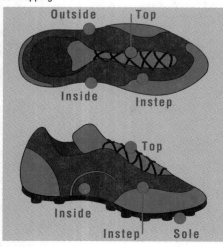

Outside   Top

Inside   Instep

Top

Inside

Instep   Sole

ball with the inside of your foot, but be sure to keep your arms out for balance and to point your nontrapping foot toward the ball.

You can also use the outside of your foot to make what is called a wedge trap. Turn your foot outward with the toes pointed down, bend your trapping knee a little, bring your trapping foot across your other foot, and wedge the ball between the outside of your foot and the ground. Skilled players can use the wedge trap to bring a ball under control, then continue running forward in one fluid movement.

The sole of the foot provides an excellent cushion for a ball traveling relatively slowly along the ground. Move your trapping foot forward to meet the ball, bending it and raising it high enough so that your sole can absorb the full impact of the ball. To maintain balance, keep your weight on your nontrapping foot.

Thigh Trap

The thigh is used to control airborne balls. Lean back slightly, bend your knee at about a 45-degree angle with the ground, and let the upper part of the thigh absorb the impact of the ball, which should then drop conveniently in front of you. Be sure to extend your arms and bend your other knee a little to maintain balance.

Chest Trap

In addition to the feet and the head, soccer players regularly use the upper chest in the course of a match. This broad surface is perfect for controlling a ball that may be awkward to head or one that bounces back off the ground. Anchor yourself firmly with your feet apart and your knees bent, extend your arms well clear of your chest, and arch your back slightly. Don't forget to relax or draw your chest back on contact—or you'll literally get the wind knocked out of you.

Head Trap

When you can't wait for an aerial ball to drop so that you can bring it under control with your chest, thigh, or foot, your only other option is to use your head (see page 29).

Passing

Very few players possess the individual skill or stamina to move the ball from one end of the field to the other on their own, so it's a lot easier if players work together. The three keys to good passing are:

1. **Accuracy** Ensuring that the ball goes directly to the feet of a teammate.

2. **Weight** Knowing how hard to hit the ball so that it will reach a teammate and then be reasonably easy to bring under control.

3. **Timing** Knowing when to hit the ball into open space so that a teammate can run to it without breaking stride.

Various kinds of passes, using different parts of the feet, can be employed in the course of a match, depending on circumstances.

Push Pass

For pinpoint accuracy over a relatively short distance—no more than 30 yards—the push pass with the inside of the foot is a soccer staple. Keep your nonkicking leg beside the ball, about four to six inches away. Bend the knee slightly and point the foot in the direction you want the pass to go. With your other leg, bend the knee, stiffen the ankle, and turn the foot to the side; then raise it off the ground, swing it back, and use the inside portion to hit the center of the ball, ensuring it rolls along the ground and doesn't bounce. Make sure you follow through, pointing your foot toward the intended target throughout the process.

Long Pass

To achieve greater power and distance with a pass, use your instep. The technique for a long pass is virtually the same as for the push pass, although it does help to approach the ball from a slight angle, as well as to use a full backswing before you strike and to follow through completely.

If you want to keep the ball on or close to the ground, concentrate on hitting the mid-portion of the ball and lean over the ball with your body as you kick it. But if you need to loft the ball, strike the lower portion of the ball and lean your body back as you kick it. In either case, keep your head steady and your eyes on the ball in order not to miskick.

You can also hit a long pass with the outside of your foot. This time the nonkicking leg should be a little behind your other leg and farther to the side than for the push pass. Bring the kicking leg across your body, following through. Depending which side of the ball you hit, your pass will swerve in a particular direction (see page 28).

Chip Pass

One of the most difficult passes to execute is the chip, which enables you to get good height on the ball as quickly as possible in order to loft it over a nearby opponent's head. The same technique can also be used to lob the ball over a goalkeeper advancing too far out from his or her goal. Place your nonkicking foot next to the ball, then bend the knee of your other foot, bring it back as far as possible (behind your thigh), and swing your foot down, striking the underside of the ball with a sharp jabbing motion, being sure not to follow through. The easiest part of the foot to use is the instep, but particularly skillful players can successfully chip a ball with either the inside or outside of their feet.

> The highest—as well as the most lopsided—score in soccer history was Arbroath 36 and Bon Accord 0 in the first round of the Scottish Cup in 1885.

Back-Heel Pass

The back-heel is a challenging pass, best used to push the ball back to a teammate behind you, often catching an opponent by surprise. To make this pass, step over the ball, sweep your foot back, and strike the ball with the broadest part of your heel as you go. Timing is crucial. Be careful not to step on the ball initially (you'll fall), then concentrate on making contact with the ball during your backswing.

Directional Passing

Whether you decide to pass the ball forward, backward, or to the side depends on your teammates' positions and how they are being marked by the opposing team's players. The **through pass** can often work extremely well for attacking players. The key is to kick the ball forward just as the player you intend it for is about to run past your opponents' last defender, thus avoiding your teammate being caught offside (see page 11). The success of this pass depends on timing both the run and the pass perfectly.

Through Pass

Soccer's equivalent of basketball's "give-and-go" is the **wall pass,** also known as a **one-two pass** in some parts of the world. The idea is for you and a teammate to exploit space behind an opponent. As soon as you pass the ball to your teammate, immediately start to run to a vacant spot on either side of the opposing player. Your teammate, acting as a "wall," will direct a one-touch pass back to you just as you sweep past the opponent you hope to catch off guard. Such a pass calls for great accuracy and timing.

One-Two Pass

Although not technically a pass, the **dummy** is an effective tactic to use during passing. If you're being

Dummy Pass

closely marked and are about to receive a pass from a teammate, you may be able to trick your opponent by, instead of trapping the ball, letting it go through your legs to a better-placed teammate.

Dribbling

Few sights in soccer are more thrilling than that of a great player weaving his or her way past a succession of opponents. The art of controlling and protecting the ball while moving it downfield is known as dribbling. It becomes particularly important when you can't find an unmarked teammate to pass to or when only a single opponent stands between you and the goal. But because the chance of giving up possession of the ball is greater with dribbling than with passing, it needs to be used selectively.

One of the most difficult skills to learn, dribbling requires the use of every part of both feet. Speed and physical resilience are other essential qualities. Important principles to remember when dribbling are:

1. Concentrating on what's happening around you, instead of watching the ball.

2. Keeping yourself well balanced at all times.

3. Being ready to change direction or pace to surprise opponents attempting to tackle you.

Moving with the Ball

The simplest way of moving forward with the ball is to tap it back and forth between the insides of both feet as you run. Strike the center of the ball to ensure it stays on the ground and push it sufficiently ahead of you (about a foot each time) so that you can maintain your stride. The ball will travel in a zigzag pattern.

To move with the ball at greater speed, you'll also need to use the outside of both feet. If you want to travel in one particular direction, you only need to propel the ball forward with one foot. Again, strike the center of the ball but use a deft touch (with no follow-through), since your momentum will do most of the work. To slow the forward move-ment of the ball at top speed, give it some back spin by kicking it much lower down.

To change direction, use the ball of your nonkicking foot as a pivot, turn to face the new direction, and propel the soccer ball with the

appropriate part of your other foot. For instance, if you're heading in a straight line and you decide to turn to the right, you can use either the inside of your left foot or the outside of the right—although the latter is much easier and quicker than the former.

Shielding the Ball

As soon as an opponent approaches while you're dribbling, it becomes important to keep your body between that person and the ball. This technique is known as shielding, or screening, the ball. Be sure to shift your body weight to whatever side is farthest from your opponent. It also helps to maintain a low center of gravity by bending your knees. Keep the ball as far from your opponent as possible, but remember that it must stay within playing distance or you'll be penalized for obstruction (see page 10).

Beating an Opponent

The real skill in dribbling comes in beating opposing players by feinting or faking, dropping your hips and shoulders to one side to make them shift direction, then pushing the ball in the opposite direction. Alternately, instead of moving to one side or the other, you may be able to "nutmeg" your opponent by pushing the ball in front of you and between his or her legs. Sometimes it takes several of these kinds of feints to fool an opponent.

Another technique is to stop the ball suddenly by placing your sole on top of it, thereby making an opponent overrun it. Even if the opponent is fast enough to react to the sudden change, you can always just nudge the ball to one side and dribble off again. Or you can fake stepping on the ball and instead of slowing down, speed up. An unexpected change in pace or direction such as this can cause great confusion. Try to make opponents commit themselves to a particular course of action and then do something different. Being able to disguise your real intentions is important—the more creative you can be, the better.

Shooting

Dribbling and passing both have an important role to play, but the ability to shoot the ball into the net transcends everything. It's also one of the most difficult skills to master.

The old adage "keep them low and in they go" still holds true. The most difficult shots for a goalkeeper to deal with are those along the ground because of the time and effort it takes to get down to them. Handling an airborne shot is much easier. And on a ground shot, there's always the chance of an unpredictable bobble or skid to catch the goalkeeper unaware. Other important keys to remember when shooting are:

1. Keeping your head steady and striking the middle or upper portion of the ball so that it stays down.

2. Staying well balanced.

3. Getting into the right position at the right time and approaching the ball from the best possible angle.

Since you rarely get much time when a shooting opportunity presents itself, quick thinking and quick reactions are essential. Although ideally you should use different parts of the feet depending on the height at which the ball comes to you and the degree of accuracy or power required, very often there isn't time to be that deliberate. The most successful shooters are the ones who are equally proficient with both feet.

Shooting with the Instep

The basic techniques for shooting are almost exactly the same as for passing. If accuracy is your principal aim, you should use the inside of your foot, but if it's power you're after, the instep must be employed. When shooting with your instep, approach the ball from a 45-degree angle and plant your nonkicking foot alongside the ball. Pulling your other foot all the way back, lean your body forward, and, keeping your toes pointed down and your ankle firm, strike the ball in one forceful, fluid movement. Be sure to follow through completely with your foot pointed in the direction of the shot. Keep your head down throughout and your eyes firmly fixed on the ball.

Swerving the Ball

Baseball pitchers have their curveballs; soccer shooters have their **banana kicks**. Making the ball swerve, bend, or spin is an important part of a player's shooting arsenal. This skill is particularly useful for a direct free kick, when the ball has to bend around a defensive wall, or when the ball must swerve past a goalkeeper who has moved off his or her line.

You can make a soccer ball swerve to the left or right depending on what part of the foot you use and what part of the ball you hit. Your aim is to slice the ball, thus imparting spin on it and making it swerve in a particular direction. If you're a left-footed player and want to bend the ball to the left, use the outside of your foot to strike the right side of the ball, but if you prefer to make it curve to the right, use the inside of your foot to hit the left side of the ball. However, if you're a right-footed player, do the reverse: to make the ball swerve left, kick the left portion of the ball with the inside of your foot, and to make it bend right, kick the right side of the ball with the outside of your foot. Since your foot kicks across the ball, your follow-through and the direction of the shot will be substantially different.

Volleying

To shoot an aerial or bouncing ball that's not the right height for heading, you'll need to use the volley. This kick is among the most difficult in soccer, mainly because contact with the ball must be minutely timed. You can either volley the ball from the side or head on, but in either case, keep your hip and knee over the ball and point your nonkicking foot in the direction of the shot. To get maximum power, use your instep. When volleying from a sideways approach, the nonkicking foot acts as a pivot. Stay upright and keep your shoulders square,

swing your foot back fully and then thrust it across your body, striking the ball firmly in the process, and follow through. For the head-on volley, draw your foot back so that it's parallel with the ground and, keeping your toes pointed firmly downward, hit the ball with full force. In both cases, the biggest problem is "ballooning" the ball into the air (kicking the ball too high), so pay special attention to keeping your head down and focusing your eyes on the ball. You can also use the inside of your foot to volley the ball for a pass or a defensive kick downfield.

The technique is very much the same for a **half-volley,** when the ball is kicked just as it hits the ground. Again, the challenge is to keep the shot low, so concentrate on leaning over and into the ball. It's also important to restrain the natural temptation to follow through fully.

Bicycle Kick

Unquestionably, soccer's most spectacular shot is the bicycle kick. If you have your back to the goal, this dramatic overhead kick is probably the only way of getting a shot on target. Only after you have fully mastered the volley should you attempt the bicycle kick, since it's potentially dangerous and requires years of practice. Many professional players go through their entire careers without perfecting it.

Begin by thrusting your nonkicking foot upward and then pushing off the ground with your other foot. As your nonkicking foot falls toward the ground, whip your other foot through the air so that you strike the middle of the ball with your instep in mid-flight, holding your ankle firm and keeping your toes pointed straight. The higher the ball is when you make contact, the lower the flight of the ball when it leaves your foot. As you follow through, absorb the impact of your fall first with the palms of your hands, then with your arms and shoulders. Be sure no opponent is close by, or the referee is likely to penalize you for dangerous kicking.

Such was the popularity of Liverpool's Scottish international striker Ian St. John in the 1960s that the following piece of graffiti became popular on walls and in men's rooms all over Britain: "Jesus saves—but St. John scores on the rebound."

Heading

Although many coaches stress the importance of keeping the ball on the ground instead of in the air—where it's harder to control—soccer will always have an aerial aspect; thus, heading continues to be an integral part of the sport. After all, it's the use of the head that adds to soccer's uniqueness.

Heading may seem unnatural and slightly unnerving for new players, so a good grounding in the proper technique is essential. Here are the key principles:

1. Use the forehead—the relatively flat, hard area above your eyes and just under the hairline—and definitely not the top of the head, or you'll be seeing stars.

2. Don't close your eyes, but instead follow the flight of the ball onto your forehead.

3. Anticipate the flight of the ball and move your head to meet it; be sure you head the ball rather than letting it hit you.

4. Keep your neck muscles tight and still, and push the upper portion of your body into the flight of the ball.

5. Extend your arms for good balance.

6. Follow through, just as you would when shooting.

When heading a ball while your feet are on the ground, spread them apart a little, if possible, to form a firm base, bend your knees, and use your legs and torso to put power into the header. However, when moving off the ground to head a ball, you must carefully read the flight of the ball and time your jump perfectly. It's best to take off on one foot, vigorously pushing up and straightening out your foot as you do so. Bend your other knee, driving it upward, and thrust both arms skyward to achieve the necessary height. Do everything possible to land on both feet.

According to RAI, the Italian television network, of the 1,162 shots at goal during the 52 matches in the 1990 World Cup finals, only 10 percent actually went into the net; 53 percent missed the goal altogether. The goal post and crossbar were hit 29 times, and only 13 of 18 penalty kicks were converted. A third of all the goals were scored in the last 15 minutes. Referees whistled for a foul almost every two minutes, and every 12th foul resulted in a yellow or red card. An average of more than eight offsides were called during each match.

Chevy Chase, famous for his slapstick comedy, learned how to fall while playing college soccer. "We were taught to roll whenever we fell on the field," he wrote in his book *Tricks of the Trade*. "And that's the basic principle behind any pratfall—you never land. You're always in motion."

Defensive Header

When heading to clear a ball (to move it downfield as far away as possible from your goal), you're usually striving for good height and distance. Since you want to head the ball upward, strike the lower part of the ball and time your jump so that you're still rising as you make the header. If you can't achieve height, aim instead for width by heading the ball sideways—but always toward the wings, never into the middle of the field.

If you're being challenged by an opposing player, use your arms and elbows to achieve as much height as possible and to power yourself above him or her, although be careful not to use them to push off of the other player or the referee will penalize you. Confidence in your ability to jump higher than your opponent as well as the skill to time your leap properly are the two most important factors.

Attacking Header

If you're heading a ball to maintain possession or with an offensive purpose in mind, you'll want it to travel downward. Hit the upper portion of the ball and get your head above the ball, striking it on its descent. Tuck your chin into your neck, keep your eyes on the ball, and be ready to rotate your torso, neck, and head in the direction you want the ball to go.

If you're heading a pass to a teammate, try and absorb as much of the impact as possible in order to soften the pace of the ball.

The most effective header at goal is one driven downward, since this is the hardest kind for a goalkeeper to handle. Properly timing both your run and your jump are critically important. On a low ball that is just too far ahead of you to be kicked, your only alternative is a **diving header.** Launch yourself full length at the ball, keeping your body parallel to the ground and your hands outstretched to cushion your landing.

On corner kicks and crosses played toward the near goal post, the closest post to the kicker, (see Chapter 6, page 19), you might not be able to head the ball on target, so instead try either a flicked or back header to redirect the ball across the goal. On a **flicked header,** use the outside portion of your forehead to deflect the ball slightly, taking a little speed off it while redirecting it somewhat. For a **back header,** use the upper portion of your forehead, just below the hairline, to glance the underside of the ball as it comes across to you. Begin by tucking your chin into your chest and timing your jump so that your head is immediately below the ball. Flick your head up and then backward on contact. The ball will be propelled a little higher than with a flicked header back across the goal.

Tackling

Tackling in soccer tends to have a negative connotation—something that's only done as a means of defense—but it's actually a positive skill since tackling a player means taking control of the ball, which puts a team back on the offensive.

Marking

Before you tackle an opponent, it helps if you are marking, or guarding, that player. By remaining close to your opponent, you may be able to prevent him or her from receiving a pass, thus removing any need for a tackle. Keep your body well balanced, spreading your legs apart and bending your knees so that you can maintain a low center of gravity and be ready to move in any direction in an instant.

The secret to good marking is positioning. You should be close enough to an opposing player so that you can intercept a pass directed his or her way or seize upon a mistake, but not so close that you can be thrown off by your opponent's sudden burst

of speed (remember that an opponent can run forward faster than you can backpedal). Be sure to remain between the person you are marking and your goal at all times. Whenever possible, force an opponent toward either of the wings instead of the middle of the field.

Intercepting

Once you have marked a player, your next goal should be to intercept any ball that comes your opponent's way. This necessitates a careful reading of the game so that you anticipate where and when the ball will be played, being sure to get there before your opponent. But don't attempt an interception unless you're certain you can reach the ball first; otherwise your opponent may be able to capitalize on your being out of position.

Jockeying

When up against a player who already has control of the ball, your first objective should be to anticipate your opponent's next move. You must be able to respond to whatever action that person decides to take. If he or she starts to dribble forward, for instance, you must be prepared to cover this move-ment by jockeying. Make sure you close off the most direct route to the goal. Turn your body in such a way that you force the player in the direction you want him or her to go. Be aware of which foot, if any, the opponent favors and then try to make him or her play the ball with the weaker foot. If possible, slow the player down by forcing him or her wide or toward a congested part of the field. Your goal is to deny your rival time and space. If you're successful, he or she may be pressured into making an error or have no alternative but to pass the ball to a teammate.

But if your opponent continues moving forward, at some point you're going to have to attempt to wrest control of the ball away by tackling. Whatever kind of tackle you decide to use, a number of basic principles apply:

1. Don't hold back; put your entire body weight behind a tackle. If you stick your leg out halfheartedly, for instance, you risk serious injury.

2. Wait until your opponent is at some disadvan-tage, such as being off-balance or on the weaker foot, before you tackle.

3. Don't over-commit yourself; keep your body well balanced.

4. Keep your eyes on the ball, not on your opponent's feet.

5. Time your tackle carefully, being sure to play the ball and not kick the legs of your opponent, or you're likely to be penalized for a foul.

6. Once you've won control of the ball, either pass it to a teammate or dribble it away quickly to prevent any chance of an opponent recovering it.

American Tom Mulroy is in *The Guinness Book of World Records* for having juggled a soccer ball 12,295 times on top of New York's Empire State Building.

Side Tackle

The technique for the side tackle is very much the same as for the front tackle, except that timing is even more crucial as you try to connect with the ball instead of your opponent's legs. Approaching an opponent from the side, either push your nontackling foot forward and use it as a pivot to bring your other foot across to block the ball from the front or prod the ball sideways using the foot farthest from your opponent. Although both of these side tackles should work, only the former is likely to result in your gaining control of the ball. With the latter, make sure you don't raise your foot and gouge your opponent's legs with your cleats.

Front Tackle

The most basic of all challenges is the front tackle, also known as the block tackle. Use the inside part of your foot, as if you were making a push pass. Bend your knees a little, hold your ankle rigid, and put all your weight into the tackle by leaning forward. Don't be afraid to lean your shoulder against your opponent's since this is perfectly legal as long as the ball is within playing distance. Swing your foot forcefully against the lower or middle part of the ball—if you aim any higher, there is a danger your foot will slide over the top of the ball and strike your opponent's shin, resulting in a possible foul.

Once you've blocked the ball, take possession of it by lifting it over your opponent's foot, pushing it to one side or the other, or even knocking it between your rival's legs. You should also be prepared to play a rebound off of the other player's foot.

Sliding Tackle

The sliding tackle is the riskiest of all tackles because unless you time it perfectly, you'll make contact with your opponent's legs before the ball and in all likelihood be called for a foul. If that happens in your own penalty area, the other team will be awarded a penalty kick. Even if you make the tackle successfully, you're normally left flat on your back and unable to resume play immediately. Nevertheless, if you're running toward an opponent from whom you need to get the ball, a sliding tackle may be your only option.

Try and approach your opponent from the side and not from behind, which is illegal and will result in an automatic foul and probably a yellow card (see page 10-11). Drop down onto the knee and calf of your nontackling leg as your other leg comes across and sweeps the ball off your opponent's foot and to the side. The key is to time your slide so that you reach the ball when it's not being directly controlled by your opponent; otherwise the player will be able to sidestep your tackle or leap over you.

Goalkeeping

Few players enjoy more individual prominence in soccer than the goalkeeper. The position is unique. In a sport dominated by use of the feet, this is the one player who must excel with his or her hands. Plus, as the last line of defense guarding a target 24 feet wide and eight feet high, goalkeepers must have all kinds of special skills. It's not always a matter of being flashy or spectacular. Many goalies have developed such all-around proficiency that they can make the job look deceptively easy. Among the most important goalkeeping qualities are:

1. **Good hand-eye coordination** Strong positional sense and solid ball-handling skills.

2. **Agility** Fast, flexible movement both in the air and on the ground.

3. **Bravery** No fear of risking personal safety when pursuing the ball.

4. **Sharp reactions** Quick reflexes to counteract all threats to the goal.

5. **Leadership** A commanding presence in the goal area and the confidence to organize defensive teammates' positioning.

Stance

When playing the position of goalie, you must be ready to respond to all kinds of situations—catching a cross ball, jumping to make a save, diving at an

opponent's feet. The basic position or stance a goalie adopts determines his or her readiness. Stand with your feet about a shoulder's width apart, your knees slightly bent, and your upper body bent forward from the waist. Hold your head steady and keep your eyes fixed on the ball at all times. Your arms should be kept slightly away from your body, with the hands outstretched and poised for action. Try to distribute your weight evenly and keep your center of gravity low so that you can move up, down, or to either side easily and quickly.

Catching the Ball

The best way for a goalie to gain control of the ball is to catch it. For this most basic of skills, position your hands around the ball with your thumbs and

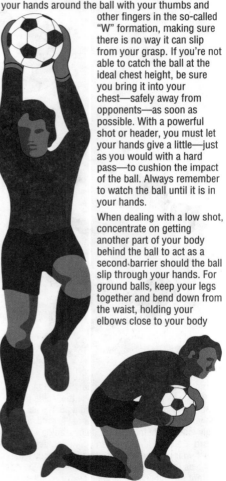

other fingers in the so-called "W" formation, making sure there is no way it can slip from your grasp. If you're not able to catch the ball at the ideal chest height, be sure you bring it into your chest—safely away from opponents—as soon as possible. With a powerful shot or header, you must let your hands give a little—just as you would with a hard pass—to cushion the impact of the ball. Always remember to watch the ball until it is in your hands.

When dealing with a low shot, concentrate on getting another part of your body behind the ball to act as a second barrier should the ball slip through your hands. For ground balls, keep your legs together and bend down from the waist, holding your elbows close to your body

and putting your hands on the ground, palms up, so that you can cradle the ball up to your chest. Better still—especially on bumpy or wet fields—drop down on one knee and, keeping your other foot in front of this knee to prevent any "hole" from opening up, put your hands onto the ground and cradle the ball up to your chest.

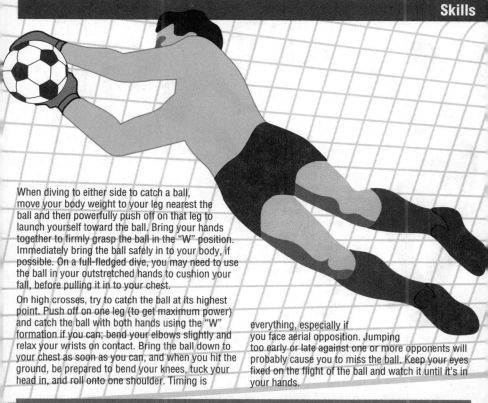

When diving to either side to catch a ball, move your body weight to your leg nearest the ball and then powerfully push off on that leg to launch yourself toward the ball. Bring your hands together to firmly grasp the ball in the "W" position. Immediately bring the ball safely in to your body, if possible. On a full-fledged dive, you may need to use the ball in your outstretched hands to cushion your fall, before pulling it in to your chest.

On high crosses, try to catch the ball at its highest point. Push off on one leg (to get maximum power) and catch the ball with both hands using the "W" formation if you can; bend your elbows slightly and relax your wrists on contact. Bring the ball down to your chest as soon as you can, and when you hit the ground, be prepared to bend your knees, tuck your head in, and roll onto one shoulder. Timing is everything, especially if you face aerial opposition. Jumping too early or late against one or more opponents will probably cause you to miss the ball. Keep your eyes fixed on the flight of the ball and watch it until it's in your hands.

Hooliganism

In recent years soccer has been blighted by a spate of hooliganism that has earned the sport unenviable headlines. In many cases the sins of a small minority of fans—if indeed they can be described as such, since many appear to be troublemakers with little real interest in the sport—have sullied the reputation of the majority. All kinds of measures have been attempted to stamp out violent incidents, such as fencing off the field, segregating fans, banning alcohol sales inside stadiums, installing closed-circuit Television cameras, and increasing police presence, but studies suggest that this is a complex social problem that defies any easy solution. Although hooliganism has become a worldwide problem, by no means limited to Britain, here's a small sampling of some of the most celebrated incidents involving British fans, notorious around the globe as the worst offenders:

1899 The English Football Association Cup semi-final replay between Sheffield United and Liverpool has to be abandoned at half-time after fans repeatedly invade the field.

1909 The Scottish Cup final between Rangers and Celtic ends with a field invasion, during which goal posts and nets are destroyed and 130 people are injured while fighting with police.

1971 Leeds United fans invade the field and a linesman is knocked unconscious by a thrown object during an English league match with West Bromwich Albion.

1974 The English Football Association Cup game between Newcastle United and Nottingham Forest is halted by a field invasion and fighting, resulting in 39 arrests, 23 hospitalizations, and 103 serious injuries.

1977 An international match between England and Scotland at London's Wembley Stadium ends with fans invading the field and causing $240,000 in damage; soon after, fences are installed at Wembley.

1985 The English Football Association Cup match between Luton Town and Millwall is interrupted by repeated fighting, resulting in 33 arrests and $40,000 in damages; British prime minister Margaret Thatcher responds by establishing a special task force to investigate hooliganism.

1990 Several thousand English fans clash with as many Italian riot police before the start of the World Cup match between England and Holland in Cagliari, resulting in more than 400 fans being detained.

1993 Before the start of the World Cup qualifying match between Holland and England, Dutch police arrest and deport some 800 English fans after they go on a rampage through the streets of Rotterdam.

Punching or Deflecting the Ball

Sometimes it's just not possible to catch a high cross—there may be too many bodies in the way— or if you try, you may drop the ball. On such occasions, punch the ball downfield with your fists. The jumping technique is the same as before, but you need to bend your elbows, clench your fists together, and then straighten your arms to make powerful contact with the ball. Be sure to punch the ball upward, aiming for as much height and distance as possible. It's always best to direct the ball toward the touchline, since this is a less dangerous part of the field than the middle. Using both fists is preferable, but a solid one-handed punch will still do the job.

When responding to a high shot directed at the goal that you know you can't catch easily, instead of punching the ball with your fists, deflect it over the crossbar with the palm and fingers of one hand. Leap for the ball just as you would for a cross and then, as you make contact with your open hand, flick your wrists to tip the ball up and over the bar safely out of play. Keep your eyes fixed on the ball, even when it goes over the bar.

You should use your palm and fingers to deflect a low shot around the goal post that you know you can't reach with both hands. Launch yourself to the side as you would for a diving catch, stretching your hand out, then flicking your wrist, to tip the ball around the post and out of play.

Positioning

Since goalkeepers are the only players allowed to handle the ball in the penalty area, it's important that you take advantage of this freedom. Always look for the best position in which to make a save.

Instead of remaining rooted to your goal line at all times, for instance, you must be prepared to leave your line when necessary. Standing on the goal line midway between the two goal posts actually offers your opponent the best scoring opportunity since he or she has a good four yards on either side of you to aim at. But the closer you get to your opponent, the more your body shields the goal, and the less chance the other player has of putting the ball past you. Eventually you reach a point where the target is completely blocked. This crucial concept is called **narrowing the angle.**

Be careful not to move so far from the goal that you give your opponent an opportunity either to chip the ball over you or to pass it to a teammate who then has a clear shot at the goal. As a general rule, don't advance any farther than the goal area unless an opponent is moving toward the goal without any of your teammates nearby to stop him.

When dealing with an opponent coming in toward the goal along the goal line, don't worry too much about approaching the player and obscuring his or her view of the goal (narrowing the angle) since it's difficult to score from that angle. Be sure to stay close to the goal line to prevent the opponent from squeezing the ball between you and the near post. Only when a player is advancing toward the goal on

Narrowing the Angle

on; don't go in head first, which could be very dangerous to your personal safety, or feet first, which could also affect your team adversely, since you'll probably be called for a foul and find yourself facing a penalty kick. If your opponent attempts to sidestep you, try and bat the ball away using your outstretched hands in one direction or your legs in the other.

Distributing the Ball

While it's easy to consider the goalkeeper as the last line of defense, it's just as easy to overlook the fact that very often he or she is the first player on offense. When making a save, receiving the ball, or restarting play with a goal kick, the goalkeeper has an opportunity to set an attacking play in motion. How he or she distributes the ball in any of these situations may well determine the success of the attack.

The main choice a goalkeeper has is whether to throw or kick the ball. For many years, goalies routinely punted the ball, but in more recent times this has become less popular. Unless the goalie is an extremely accurate kicker and has unmarked teammates stationed downfield, there's only a 50-50 chance that his or her side will retain possession of the ball after the kick. Instead, the emphasis has switched to an accurately thrown pass that enables the goalkeeper's team to keep the ball and build an attack.

his or her own without any teammates close by should you move out to take action.

On a cross from the wing, avoid the temptation to station yourself too close to the near post but instead hang back a little toward the far post (it's always much easier and quicker to move to the near post than it is to backtrack to the far post).

When you do come off your line to go one-on-one with an opponent closing in on the goal, it takes great courage to dive at the player's feet for the ball. As you approach, try to use body movements and fakes to force him or her toward the touchline or into a position that affords the worst possible shooting angle. But if the opponent keeps coming, you'll have to go after him or her. Crouch down, keeping yourself low to the ground, and attempt to get as much of your body as possible in front of the ball. Throw your legs sideways and try to wrest control of the ball with the palms and fingers of your hands. If you do get the ball, clutch it to your chest immediately, though in all likelihood you'll probably have to settle for knocking it away. Approach side

Houston Rockets basketball star Hakeem Olajuwon played as a goalie on the Lagos Stars youth soccer team that reached the semi-finals of the prestigious Dallas Cup tournament in 1982. "Goalkeeping develops skills that directly relate to basketball," says Olajuwon. "How to catch the ball with soft hands, how to move your body laterally and help make your reflexes more sharp . . . playing goalkeeper helped me progress quickly once I began playing basketball."

The most accurate throw of all is the **underarm roll** along the ground to a nearby teammate, who then has a relatively easy job of trapping the ball. The technique is exactly the same as in bowling. Hold the underside of the ball with your hand, move your arm back, take a step forward with the leg opposite your throwing hand, and swing this hand forward, releasing the ball when your arm is perpendicular to the ground. Follow through in the direction of the throw.

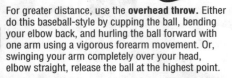

For greater distance, use the **overhead throw.** Either do this baseball-style by cupping the ball, bending your elbow back, and hurling the ball forward with one arm using a vigorous forearm movement. Or, swinging your arm completely over your head, elbow straight, release the ball at the highest point.

Argentinian World Cup captain Diego Maradona received a 15-month worldwide soccer ban in 1991 after testing positive for cocaine while playing for Napoli, his Italian club team.

It's not all bright lights in the world of international soccer—at least not in impoverished Albania. When Northern Ireland traveled to Tirana for a 1994 World Cup qualifying match, the players discovered their hotel had no running water, the toilets didn't work, and cardboard covered the windows instead of glass. And after a World Cup qualifier against Denmark, Albanian officials agonized over how to replace three shirts that had been given up during the traditional exchange of shirts at the end of the match.

Moshoud Abiola, the reputed winner of Nigeria's 1993 presidential election (the results were later annulled by the military), promised each of the players on the national team a $100,000 bonus if the country qualified for the 1994 World Cup. They did.

If you want to get the ball downfield as quickly as possible (especially when time is running out), you'll need to **kick** it. To punt the ball while it's in the air, hold it in both hands, drop it in front of you, take one step forward, and kick it with your instep before it hits the ground. Or, for a little less trajectory (especially on a blustery day) and consequently a little more accuracy, drop-kick the ball using the same technique as punting except striking it as it hits the ground.

Since 1992, when a new rule was introduced preventing goalkeepers from handling any ball kicked to them by a teammate, goalies have been forced to use their feet more than ever before. Instead of just kicking the ball away wildly, goalkeepers are now learning good trapping and passing skills.

Running off the Ball

Studies show that during a soccer match each player has possession of the ball for no more than five minutes. Most of the remaining 85 minutes are spent moving around the field without the ball. This movement is called running off the ball and can have just as profound an impact on the outcome of a match as running with the ball.

Even if a teammate has the ball some distance away from you, there's no excuse for standing around waiting for something to happen in your part of the field. Since a soccer ball can be kicked in an instant from one end of the field to the other, you must always be ready for a sudden change in the action that brings you directly into play. You'll need to be constantly on the move to take care of such basic tactical considerations as marking an opponent, avoiding being caught offside, trying to catch the other team offside, and so on.

Sometimes you should actually run in a completely different direction from where the ball is in order to draw an opponent who's marking you away from the action. This can create more space for your

Overlap Run

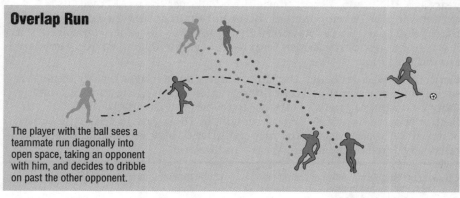

The player with the ball sees a teammate run diagonally into open space, taking an opponent with him, and decides to dribble on past the other opponent.

Diagonal Run

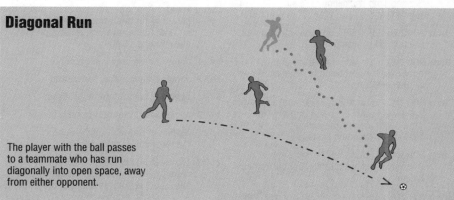

The player with the ball passes to a teammate who has run diagonally into open space, away from either opponent.

teammates who have the ball. This type of decoy play can be especially effective during free kicks to confuse the other team.

The main purpose of off-the-ball running, however, is to get into position to receive a pass. This is known as **supporting the play.** Often it's a matter of being in the right place at the right time. For instance, if you're playing as the right midfielder, you should be ready to run forward when your teammate on the right wing starts attacking down the flank. One such technique might be an **overlap run,** where you move past the right winger and get into a clear, onside position downfield so you can receive the ball. Another technique is a **diagonal run** across the field into open space to receive a pass. Both kinds of runs can catch opposing players off guard, but they depend on you perfectly timing your run.

History

Though historians believe a game resembling soccer was played in both China and Egypt at least 4,000 years ago, the modern sport now enjoyed all over the world owes its existence to the development of soccer in Britain during the course of more than 1,700 years. Soccer was dutifully exported to the American colonies, as it was to the rest of the British Empire and eventually almost every country around the globe.

Contrary to popular belief, the United States has a longer history of playing soccer than any country except Britain, as shown in the following timeline. Only a handful of English clubs existed when the Oneida Football Club in Boston became America's first soccer club in 1862. And in 1885, the United States and Canada became the first countries to play an international match outside of England, Scotland, Wales, and Ireland.

Circa 2500 BC First mention of ancient ball game of *tsu chu* in China—*tsu* meaning "kicking" and *chu* denoting "a stuffed ball of animal skin."

Circa 2000 BC Ball juggling is depicted on wall painting in Egyptian tomb.

Circa 600 BC First record of Greek game of *episkyros*, the goal being to move a ball over an opponent's line.

Circa 600 BC–circa AD 300 *Kemari*, an ancient ball game similar to soccer, is played in Japan, with players attempting to kick a ball between two bamboo posts.

Circa 600 BC–circa AD 400 Ball game of *harpastum* is played throughout the Roman Empire.

Circa AD 200 Celtic tribes in England and France adapt *harpastum* for their own game, which supposedly involves kicking around the skulls of defeated Roman soldiers.

Circa 600-1550 Mayan ball game of *pokyah* is played on courts throughout modern-day Mexico, Honduras, El Salvador, and Belize using only the feet, legs, hips, and elbows.

Circa 1100-1800 Game of *le soule*, a forerunner of soccer, flourishes in France.

1175 **William Fitzstephen,** an English monk, makes the first literary mention of "the famous game of ball" when he refers to soccer matches played in England on Shrove Tuesday.

1280 Soccer player in England dies after falling on his dagger.

Circa 1300 Italian explorers report seeing a form of soccer being played in China.

1314 **Edward II** bans soccer in England, complaining that "there is a great noise in the city caused by hustling over large balls from which many evils might arise which God forbid."

1349 **Edward III** bans soccer in England because it interferes with his citizens' need for archery practice.

1389 **Richard II** bans soccer in England once again.

Circa 1400-1700 *Giuco del calcio Fiorentino* is played by the aristocracy in Florence's Piazza di Santa Croce, involving kicking, passing, and carrying a ball.

1424 **James I** bans soccer in Scotland.

1457 **James II** bans soccer in Scotland.

1491 **James IV** bans soccer in Scotland.

1497 James IV actually starts to play soccer.

1527 **Statute of Galway** legitimizes soccer in Ireland but bans other sports.

1572 **Elizabeth I** bans soccer in London in response to a report that sometimes players' "necks are broken, sometimes their backs or legs, sometimes their noses gush out blood, and sometimes their eyes are put out."

1581 English headmaster claims soccer "strengtheneth and brawneth the whole body…. It is good to drive down the stone and gravel from the bladder and the kidneys."

1583 **Philip Stubbs,** a Puritan pamphlet writer, describes soccer in *The Anatomie of Abuses* as featuring "murder, brawling, contortion, quarrel kicking, homicide, and great effusion of blood."

1605 Soccer is officially legalized in England.

1609 Match played at Jamestown, Virginia, is the first documented mention of soccer in the New World.

Circa 1620 Organized soccer games are played at Trinity and St. John's Colleges in Cambridge, England.

1634 According to **William Wood,** an early colonist in the New World, "the Indians played football [soccer] during the summer months with a varying number of players," and he was impressed by "their swift footmanship, their strange manipulation of the ball," but nevertheless believed that "one Englishman could beat 10 Indians at football."

1681 **Charles II** allows his servants to play soccer.

Circa 1700-present *Aqsaqtuk,* a game closely resembling soccer on ice, is played by Eskimos in Canada and Alaska.

1814 Soccer matches are played at England's Harrow School, with each team restricted to 11 players.

1815 Scottish soccer match between Selkirk and Yarrow is watched by author **Sir Walter Scott,** a great Selkirk fan.

1823 **William Webb Ellis** picks up the ball and runs with it at **Rugby School,** thus pioneering the development of rugby.

1827 Harvard University holds its first annual soccer match (on "Bloody Monday").

Circa 1830 **Harrow School Rules** ban "hacking" (kicking an opponent's leg) and passing the ball by hand.

1840 Intramural tournaments of *ballown* (using hands and feet) are first played at Princeton.

1845 First reference to a referee—at England's Eton School.

1848 **Cambridge University Rules** are drawn up for a "dribbling" version of soccer (goals are awarded for balls kicked between posts and under a string, and running with the ball in one's hands is banned).

1851 Annual soccer match between freshmen and sophomores is formally established at Yale University.

1857 **Sheffield Football Club,** England's first soccer team, is founded.

1860 Harvard bans soccer because of violent play.

1862 **Notts County,** the oldest club still in the English Football League, is founded. The **Oneida Football Club,** the first organized U.S. soccer club, is founded in Boston, Massachusetts. The emphasis is on "dribbling."

1863 In England, the **Football Association** is formed. It establishes "The Laws of the Game," the first nationally recognized set of rules.

1865 Tape is stretched across top of goal posts for first time.

1866 Handling the ball is prohibited for all players except the goalkeeper.

Turkey so feared British influence at the turn of the century that a group of British soccer players touring the country was arrested in 1895. The team's shirts were said to be uniforms, its soccer balls cannonballs, and its set of rules subversive literature.

1867 South America's first soccer team, **Buenos Aires Football Club,** is founded as an offshoot of the Buenos Aires Cricket Club.

1868 The **Montreal Football Club** becomes the first Canadian soccer team to play under England's 1863 Football Association rules.

1869 Introduction of the goal kick. First intercollegiate soccer match is played (with a round ball) between Princeton and Rutgers.

1870 Britons introduce soccer to Germany and Australia.

1871 **Rugby Football Union** is founded in England, firmly establishing the difference between soccer and rugby.

1872 The **Football Association Challenge Cup (F.A. Cup)** is first contested in England. England and Scotland play world's first international match. Britons introduce soccer to France. The corner kick is instigated.

1873 Free kick is introduced to punish handling of the ball. **Princeton, Rutgers, Yale,** and **Columbia** formulate their own set of rules (including a ban on handling the ball) based on England's 1863 Football Association rules. Eton Players from England play Yale in first Anglo-American soccer match. **Canadian Football Association (CFA)** is formed.

1874 Shinguard is invented and patented. Harvard plays McGill University of Montreal (with an oval ball) in first universally recognized American football match.

1875 Crossbar replaces tape. Yale renounces soccer and plays American football match against Harvard.

1876 **Harvard, Princeton,** and **Columbia** form the **Intercollegiate Football Association,** dealing soccer a mortal blow in the U.S.

1878 First floodlit game is played in Sheffield, England. Umpires begin using whistles.

1879 First African soccer club, **Pietermaritzburg County,** is founded in Natal, South Africa.

1880 Earliest Australasian soccer club is founded in Sydney. Soccer gets first exposure in sub-Saharan Africa when a Jamaican introduces the sport to the Gold Coast (now Ghana). Football Association sanctions use of shinguards.

1882 England, Scotland, Wales, and Ireland form **International Football Association Board** to regulate rule changes. Introduction of two-handed throw-in.

1884 First international tournament played by England, Scotland, Wales, and Ireland. Founding of **American Football Association (AFA),** first U.S. governing body for soccer.

1885 Professionals are allowed to play in F.A. Cup and English international matches. System of two points for a win and one point for a tie is introduced. First North American international match is played between the U.S. and Canada in Newark, New Jersey.

1887 Britons introduce soccer to Russia.

1888 **Football League,** the world's first national league, starts play in England.

1890 Introduction of penalty kick. New York soccer clubs withdraw from AFA and form **American Amateur Football Association (AAFA).**

1891 Football League introduces referees and linesmen to replace umpires. Introduction of center spot, center circle, goal nets, and penalty kick. Argentina introduces South America's first domestic league championship. U.S.-Canadian team becomes the first foreign team to tour Britain.

1894 Britons introduce soccer in Brazil. **American League of Professional Football Clubs** is formed by owners of professional baseball teams in Boston, New York, Washington, Baltimore, Philadelphia, and Brooklyn, but after lopsided 10-1 defeat of Washington by Baltimore, the *Washington Post* reports: "Baltimore's professional football team found Washington about as easy to beat as the baseball Orioles found the Senators during the baseball season," and within three weeks the League folds.

1896 Soccer is played as an unofficial demonstration sport at first modern Olympic Games in Athens. Referees are allowed to penalize players by calling fouls. Length of a match is fixed at 90 minutes.

1898 Introduction of first players' union in England. Beginning of **Calcutta League** in India.

1899 Formation of **Milan Cricket and Football Club** (later renamed AC Milan).

1902 First non-British international match is played between Austria and Hungary. Introduction of halfway line. Present goal area and penalty area are introduced. Women's clubs are refused admission into Football Association; women's team from Preston, England, tours the U.S.

Chicago's Soldier Field underwent an $18 million structural renovation to host the opening ceremonies of the 1994 World Cup.

Sweden made a stunning international debut in 1908, drubbing neighboring Norway 11-3 at Göteborg in its first match ever.

1903 Introduction of advantage rule.

1904 **Fédération Internationale de Football Association (FIFA),** the world governing body for soccer, is founded by France, Belgium, Denmark, the Netherlands, Spain, Sweden, and Switzerland. Canada wins Olympic Games exhibition soccer tournament in St. Louis.

1905 Argentina and Uruguay compete in first South American international match. Introduction of drop ball.

1906 England's famous **Corinthians Football Club** tours the U.S.

1908 First official soccer tournament is played at the Olympic Games in London.

1909-1921 The **Eastern** (later **National**) **League** is contested by clubs in New York, New Jersey, and Pennsylvania.

1911 **Stanford University** starts varsity soccer program, the first of its kind west of the Mississippi.

1912 Goalkeepers are prohibited from handling the ball outside their own penalty area. **Dominion of Canada Football Association** replaces CFA. **Connaught Cup** play begins for top Canadian clubs.

1913 Philippines plays China in first Asian international match. Opposing players must be 10 yards (instead of six yards) away from the ball at free kicks and corner kicks. **United States Football Association (USFA)** is formed from the AAFA (also incorporating the AFA).

1914 USFA becomes a member of FIFA. Brooklyn wins first **National Open Challenge Cup** competition for major U.S. clubs.

1916 **Confederacíon Sudamericana de Fútbol (CONMEBOL)** is founded to administer soccer in South America. Launching of **South American Championship** (now known as **Copa América**), the first competition for the region's national teams. Africa's first domestic league championship begins play in Morocco. U.S. beats Sweden 3-2 and ties with Norway 1-1 in its first overseas international matches.

1920 **Australian Football Association** is founded. Women's international match between England and France attracts crowd of 10,000.

1921 The first U.S. professional league, the **American Soccer League (ASL),** begins play.

1923 Egypt becomes first African country to join FIFA.

1924 U.S. plays in Olympic Games soccer tournament for first time. Canadian national team makes its first overseas tour, to Australia.

1925 Offside rule is changed, allowing two defenders between an attacker and the goal line instead of three.

1926 Crowd of 35,000 for match between **German-American Football Association All-Stars** and Austria's **Hakoah Vienna** in New York sets U.S. attendance record (unbroken until mid-1970s).

1927 First radio broadcast of a soccer match— Arsenal vs. Sheffield United in England.

1929 Goalkeepers must remain stationary on their goal lines during a penalty kick.

1930 Uruguay hosts first **World Cup** soccer tournament; the U.S. reaches the semi-finals.

1932 Substitutions are allowed for international matches.

1933 Numbers appear on soccer shirts for first time. ASL is reconstituted after collapsing in the late 1920s.

1935 First national youth soccer tournament takes place in the U.S.

1937 First television broadcast of a soccer match—Preston North End vs. Sunderland in English F.A. Cup final. Permissible weight of ball increased by one ounce.

1938 **Confederación Centroamericana y del Caribe de Fútbol (CCCF)** is founded to administer soccer in Central America and the Caribbean.

1939 U.S. joins the **North American Confederation,** a forerunner of the present CONCACAF. Indoor soccer is played for first time at Madison Square Garden in New York.

1941 **National Soccer Coaches Association** is formed, covering U.S. collegiate soccer.

1945 USFA is renamed **United States Soccer Football Association (USSFA).**

1946-1950 FIFA expels Germany and Japan following World War II.

1948 U.S. suffers record 11-0 defeat against Norway in Oslo.

1950 U.S. shocks the world with 1-0 win against England in the World Cup at Belo Horizonte, Brazil.

1951 Obstruction becomes an indirect free kick offense.

1954 Founding of **Union of European Football Associations (UEFA)** and **Asian Football Confederation (AFC).**

1955 **European Cup** and **Fairs Cup** (the latter now known as **UEFA Cup**) are both launched.

1956 **Asian Cup** is contested for first time.

1957 Newly formed **Confédération Africaine de Football (CAF)** launches **African Cup of**

Nations. Unofficial **European Women's Football Championship** takes place in West Berlin. Canada plays its first home international match, against the U.S.

1958 **European Nations' Cup** (now known as **European Championship**) is launched.

1959 **National Collegiate Athletic Association (NCAA)** sanctions first national soccer championship in the U.S.

1960 Introduction of South America's **Copa Libertadores** and the **European Cup Winners' Cup.** Winners of European Cup and Copa Libertadores contest **Intercontinental Cup** (now known as **World Club Championship**) for first time. Eleven foreign teams and an American all-star team begin play in the **International Soccer League (ISL).**

1961 **Confederación Norte-Centroamericana y del Caribe de Fútbol (CONCACAF)** supersedes CCCF by incorporating North America. **Eastern Canada Professional Soccer League (ECPSL)** makes its debut.

1964 **African Cup of Champion Clubs** begins play. FIFA expels South Africa. **American Youth Soccer Organization (AYSO)** is founded.

1965 Founding of **Oceania Football Confederation (OFC).** ISL folds.

1966 World Cup final between England and West Germany is televised in the U.S. ECPSL folds.

1967 FIFA allows two substitutions in any international match. **United Soccer Association (USA)** and **National Professional Soccer League (NPSL)** begin two rival leagues, both heavily reliant on foreign players. NPSL gains network television contract with CBS.

1968 Yellow and red cards are introduced at Olympic soccer tournament in Mexico City. England's Football Association officially recognizes women's soccer. USA and NPSL merge to create **North American Soccer League (NASL).**

1969 "Fútbol War" breaks out between El Salvador and Honduras as a result of tensions over the rights of Salvadoran settlers in Honduras; riots, precipitated by soccer matches between the countries, lead to war, in which thousands are killed and injured. Former Welsh international **Phil Woosnam** becomes NASL executive director.

1971 FIFA expels Chad for repeated nonpayment of annual dues. FIFA allows naming of five substitutes. Unofficial **World Championship for Women** takes place in Mexico City. **Women's Football Association** is founded in England. **New York Cosmos** join NASL.

1972 Brazil celebrates 150 years of independence by holding (and winning) **Copa Independencia do Brazil.** NASL organizes first college draft. New York Cosmos wins its first NASL title.

1973 American-born **Kyle Rote, Jr.**, wins NASL scoring title and Rookie of the Year title. NASL adapts offside rule by changing demarcation from halfway line to a line 35 yards from goal line.

1974 Brazilian **João Havelange** becomes president of FIFA. USSFA changes its name to **United States Soccer Federation (USSF).** NASL eliminates draws by resolving tied matches with penalty kicks. Former basketball star **Bob Cousy** becomes commissioner of ASL.

1975 FIFA readmits China. **African Cup Winners Cup** begins play. **Asian Women's Football Tournament** is officially sanctioned in Hong Kong. Soccer great **Pelé** comes out of retirement to play for New York Cosmos in NASL. NASL championship game is renamed **Soccer Bowl.**

1976 NASL stipulates that one North American-born player must always be on the field. New York Cosmos drops its first name and becomes the Cosmos.

1977 Soviet Union wins FIFA's inaugural **Under-20 World Cup.** German star **Franz Beckenbauer** joins Pelé at Cosmos and helps the club, along with Pelé, win Soccer Bowl. Record crowd of 77,691 watches Cosmos beat Fort Lauderdale Strikers 8-3 at Giants Stadium, New Jersey. Pelé retires for a second time. NASL introduces "shoot-out" to resolve ties.

1978 Cosmos win Soccer Bowl again. **Major Indoor Soccer League** (later renamed **Major Soccer League**) begins play in the U.S.

1979 Ayatollah Khomeini bans soccer in Iran. Two European stars join NASL—**Johan Cruyff** with the Los Angeles Aztecs and **Gerd Müller** with the Fort Lauderdale Strikers. ABC agrees to televise nine NASL matches, including Soccer Bowl.

1980 World Club Championship is renamed **Toyota Cup** and permanently moved to Tokyo, Japan.

1981 Fiftieth anniversary of first World Cup is celebrated by **Copa de Oro** tournament for all previous winners (won by host team Uruguay). NCAA sanctions first national women's soccer championship.

1983 FIFA rejects U.S. bid to host 1986 World Cup. **Team America** is formed.

1984 ASL folds. U.S. hosts Olympic Games soccer tournament. **American Indoor Soccer Association** (later renamed **National Professional Soccer League**) begins indoor play and the **United Soccer League (USL)** is formed.

1985 Riot leaves 39 fans dead at **Brussels' Heysel Stadium** before start of European Cup Final between Liverpool and Juventus, and as a result English club teams are banned from European cup competitions. Nigeria becomes first African nation ever to win a world title by triumphing in FIFA's inaugural **Under-17 World Cup.** NASL and USL both fold.

1986 **Western Soccer Alliance** (later renamed **Western Soccer League**) begins play in the United States. Canada qualifies for World Cup finals in Mexico.

1987 **Canadian Soccer League (CSL)** begins play.

1988 FIFA awards 1994 World Cup to the U.S. The **American Soccer League** is revived once more and begins play in the eastern U.S.

1989 At Hillsborough Stadium in Sheffield, England, 95 fans die before start of English F.A. Cup semi-final when they try to crash an unopened gate. U.S. finishes fourth in Under-20 World Cup in Saudi Arabia. U.S. qualifies for 1990 World Cup finals. U.S. wins bronze medal in first **FIFA Five-a-Side World Indoor Championship.**

1990 European cup competition ban is lifted on all English club teams except Liverpool. Offside rule is amended so that an attacker in line with the penultimate defender is now onside. U.S. competes in World Cup. Western Soccer League and American Soccer League merge to form **American Professional Soccer League (APSL).**

1991 FIFA suspends Iraq after invasion of Kuwait. Lithuania, Latvia, and Estonia are recognized as FIFA members. USSF assumes its present name of **U.S. Soccer.** U.S. wins inaugural **CONCACAF Gold Cup** and FIFA's first official **Women's World Cup** in China.

1992 FIFA readmits Chad and South Africa. Olympic soccer tournament becomes official World Under-23 Championship. New rule is introduced banning goalkeepers from handling passes kicked by teammates. Yugoslavia is banned from 1994 World Cup qualifying tournament. **Intercontinental Championship** makes its debut. MSL folds. U.S. wins silver medal in FIFA Five-a-Side World Indoor Championship.

1993 **J-League** begins play in Japan. Agreement is reached to add women's soccer as a medal sport at 1996 Summer Olympics in Atlanta. CSL folds. **Continental Indoor Soccer League (CISL)** begins play. U.S. shocks England again with a 1-0 win in **U.S. Cup.** **U.S. International Soccer League (USISL)** receives Division III status by U.S. Soccer. FIFA approves **Major League Soccer,** a 12-team professional league scheduled to begin play in April 1995.

1994 U.S. hosts World Cup for the first time.

World Soccer

Soccer is truly an international sport. Unlike America's two favorite pastimes—football, which isn't played at all outside of North America, and baseball, whose influence hasn't reached much beyond Canada, Latin America, and parts of Asia—soccer has captured the attention and interest of countries across the globe. The explanation is simple: the rapid growth of the game at the turn of the century coincided with the rise of colonialism. Soccer's first exporters were the British, followed by the French, the Spanish, and the Portuguese, then the Dutch, the Belgians, and the Germans. Fanning out all over the world, the colonial powers established soccer as the sport of choice wherever they went.

In the 20th century, soccer's popularity has exposed it to the tribulations of international politics. The World Cup is a perfect example. In 1957, all African and Asian countries scheduled to play Israel in World Cup qualifying matches withdrew in protest. Twelve years later, World Cup qualifying games between El Salvador and Guatemala were used as a pretext to fan the flames of existing border tensions, producing the so-called Fútbol War. Then in 1974, the Soviet Union refused to play a World Cup match against Chile, claiming the soccer stadium in Santiago was being used as a prison by Chilean strongman Augusto Pinochet, and in 1989, General Khaddafi of Libya canceled a World Cup game against Algeria, with 70,000 spectators already in the stadium in Tripoli, saying that an air strike by the United States was imminent.

Worldwide Competitions

Although the idea for the **World Cup** was first suggested in 1904, it took another 26 years before the tournament became a reality. Until then, soccer looked to the **Olympic Games** to crown its world champions. With the sport in its infancy in most countries, the first three Olympiads only recognized soccer on an exhibition basis. The first official Olympic soccer tournament was at the London Games in 1908. Six European nations entered the competition, with a team of amateur players from England duly confirming the country's long-perceived supremacy. The number of competing countries gradually increased in subsequent Olympics, but not until the appearance of Uruguay, Egypt, and the United States in 1924 could the tournament seriously claim to be a world championship. Uruguay's victory that year and four years later at the Amsterdam Games left no doubt that it was the world's best team—and this was only underlined when essentially the same Uruguayan team won the inaugural World Cup in 1930.

The Olympic soccer tournament has lived in the World Cup's shadow ever since. As professional soccer spread throughout the globe, more and more countries were unable to send their best teams to an event that supposedly enshrined the ideals of amateurism—not that this stopped the state-sponsored teams of Eastern Europe, who won every tournament from 1952 to 1980. Only Hungary's "Magic Magyars," who triumphed in the 1952 Helsinki Olympics, could be considered true world champions. Virtually the same Hungarian team obliterated all major opposition to reach the 1954 World Cup final, only to be beaten by West Germany in one of soccer's great upsets of all time.

At the 1980 Moscow Games, the **Fédération Internationale de Football Association (FIFA)** introduced a new rule preventing any player who had appeared in a World Cup game from playing in the Olympics, but this only served to further downgrade the importance of the Olympic soccer tournament. After much haggling with frustrated Olympic officials, FIFA finally agreed not only to lift this ban in 1992, but also to firmly establish the Olympic tournament as the official world championship for national teams in the under-23 age group. However, at the 1996 Olympic Games in Atlanta, each team will be allowed to field three players over the age of 23.

In its continuing zeal to promote soccer's worldwide popularity, FIFA decided to organize a World Youth Cup for national teams in the under-20 age group in 1977—subsequently known as the **Under-20 World Cup.** And such was the tournament's success that eight years later the **Under-17 World Cup** made its debut. Both competitions are held every two years. Although there has been great controversy about the advisability of introducing competitive soccer at such a young age—not to mention accusations of over-age players being illegally used by some teams—the Under-17 World Cup has been well received because of its surprisingly high standard of play, especially among the African nations, who've won three of the five tournaments held so far. Africa has not yet been able to reproduce this success at the Under-20 level. Developing nations are far more equitably represented in the Youth World Cups than they are in the "Senior" World Cup. For instance, of the 16 countries that contested the 1993 Under-20 championship, six were from Europe, three from South America, two each from North and Central America, Africa, and Asia, and one from Oceania.

FIFA's thirst for yet more international tournaments was slaked in 1993 with the introduction of the **Intercontinental Cup,** which brought together the champions of four FIFA confederations—Argentina as Copa América winners, the United States as Gold Cup winners, Côte d'Ivoire as African Nations Cup winners, and Saudi Arabia as Asian Cup winners.

In 1991, FIFA acknowledged the surge in the number of female soccer players by organizing the first **Women's World Cup.** A grand total of 31 countries began qualifying play, resulting in 12 nations—five from Europe, three from Asia, and one each from South America, Africa, Oceania, and North and Central America—gathering in China for an historic tournament that saw the United States eventually crowned as world champions. Just like its male counterpart, the Women's World Cup takes place every four years.

Professional club soccer, in which domestic teams play one another, occurs in almost every nation in the world. Most countries have two different kinds of competition: a league championship, in which all the clubs compete on a round-robin basis, and a cup tournament, during which the clubs play single-elimination matches until a winner emerges.

Each country has a national team that selects the best players from the clubs to compete internationally. Consequently, most of the world's top stars play soccer at both the club and national level.

Europe

The fact that modern soccer originated in Britain, quickly took root across the Channel in France, and then steadily spread all over the rest of the continent ensured that the sport remained Eurocentric for many years. Significantly, soccer's world governing body came into being in 1904 in Paris and is still known by its French title and acronym—the Fédération Internationale de Football Association (FIFA). Such was the European stranglehold on FIFA that not until 1954 did the nations of Europe feel any need to organize their own regional organization, the **Union of European Football Associations (UEFA).** Europe's continuing dominance over world soccer is reflected in the number of spots that FIFA allots in the World Cup finals. In 1994, Europe filled 13 of the 24 spots, compared to four for South America, three for Africa, two for Asia, and two for North and Central America.

Europe is home to the world's second largest soccer tournament after the World Cup. The **European Championship,** open to all of UEFA's member nations, made its debut in 1958 and like its illustrious counterpart is held every four years—the two tournaments alternate, one taking place every two years. The European Championship's format is also very similar to that of the World Cup: a qualifying competition takes place, then the championship itself is hosted by one of the member countries. In 1996, the European Championship will double in size from eight to 16 nations.

The continent also boasts three major club competitions. Most celebrated of all is the **European**

Champion Clubs' Cup—more commonly known as the **European Cup**—contested by the winners of the league championship in each of UEFA's member countries. First held in 1955, it is now regarded as Europe's premier club competition. Second in importance is the **European Cup Winners' Cup,** which began in 1960, for the winners of the single-elimination cup tournament held in each country. And, finally, there's the **UEFA Cup** (initially known as the **Inter Cities Fairs Cup** when it debuted in 1958) for the remainder of Europe's best club teams; the number of teams each country can enter depends upon that country's past performances in all three club competitions. In 1993, for instance, Germany was represented by the maximum four clubs, while Cyprus only had one entrant. All three competitions are played at home and away (one game each in the hometown of each team), on a single-elimination basis, with the aggregate (total) score from the two matches determining which club advances to the next round. If the aggregate score is tied, the team scoring the most goals in its away match advances; if this doesn't produce a winner, a penalty shootout is held. Several years ago, the European Cup abolished the quarter-final and semi-final stages, replacing them with two groups, each of four teams, playing round-robin matches to determine two group winners, who then meet in the final.

In 1960, UEFA decided to challenge its South American counterpart to an annual match between the winners of the European Cup and the "best club team" in South America. This was the spark that produced the **Copa Libertadores,** the South American equivalent of the European Cup, which enabled the champions of Europe and South America to meet in what was initially christened the **Intercontinental Cup** but soon came to be known—with much hyperbole—as the **World Club Championship.** For its first 20 years, the two-leg home-and-away championship produced a series of increasingly violent matches that eventually resulted in some European clubs refusing to take part. Only since 1980, when Toyota of Japan agreed to sponsor the event as a single match in neutral Tokyo, has the newly renamed **Toyota Cup** begun to regain some of its original appeal.

Denmark

Soccer caught on surprisingly early in Denmark, with the country's plucky amateurs reaching the final of both the 1908 and 1912 Olympics, only to be defeated each time by the powerhouse players of England. Unfortunately, amateurism then took such a hold on the sport that Denmark became a soccer backwater for the next 60 years. Not until the late 1970s did the glory days return, with a slew of outstanding players leaving Denmark to fine-tune their skills in Europe's top leagues before returning home to play for their country. A Danish semi-final appearance in the 1984 European Championship was followed by an impressive run in the 1986 World Cup—the first time Denmark had ever qualified for the finals—and a stunning upset in the

1992 European Championship, when the country received a spot at the last minute replacing banished Yugoslavia and promptly went on to win the tournament. Danish league (club) soccer still has a long way to go to emulate the success of the national team, however; no club has even made it to a major European final, let alone won a competition.

Record

World Cup: Never gone beyond second round

Olympic Games: Finalists 1908, 1912; third place 1948

European Championship: Winner 1992; semi-finalist 1984

European Cup: No club has ever gone beyond quarter-finals

European Cup Winners Cup: No club has ever gone beyond quarter-finals

UEFA Cup: No club has ever gone beyond semi-finals

Top Players

Preben Elkjaer-Larsen One of Denmark's most colorful players, he scored a notable hat trick (three goals) in the 1986 World Cup against Uruguay, and finished his international career with 38 goals in 69 international appearances.

Michael Laudrup An exciting striker, Laudrup first came to the fore in the 1984 European Championship, when he outscored all other players, then made a big impact at the 1986 World Cup, where he was Denmark's leading goal-scorer. After joining the star-studded Juventus team of Italy that won the 1985 European Cup, he helped Barcelona win the European Cup in 1992.

Peter Schmeichel A remarkable goalkeeper, noted for his spectacular saves, strong punting ability, and superb distribution skills, Schmeichel came into the international limelight after his move from his local team, Broendby, to England's Manchester United in 1991. The following year, he put on an incredible show during Denmark's European Championship triumph.

Allan Simonsen Probably the greatest of the "great" Danes during the late '70s and early '80s, this compact striker scored 21 goals for his country and made quite a name for himself with West Germany's Borussia Mönchengladbach, helping the team win two UEFA Cup finals (in 1975 and 1979). He was recognized as European Footballer of the Year in 1977.

England

As the birthplace of modern soccer, England stayed in the forefront of the sport for most of this century, emerging victorious from the first two Olympic tournaments and reaching its zenith in 1966 by winning the World Cup. But in recent years, this dominance has begun to erode, culminating in the country's failure to qualify for the 1994 World Cup.

Even England's league championship, revered as the most competitive in the world for almost its entire history, has lost some of its luster, although the **Football Association Cup** (popularly known as the **F.A. Cup**), the world's first single-elimination club tournament, remains untarnished. English teams enjoyed an outstanding record in all three European club competitions until 1985, when hooliganism overshadowed play during the European Cup final in Brussels (see page 53), leading to England's banishment from all future European Cup tournaments. Since the ban was lifted in 1990 (for all clubs except Liverpool), the English clubs haven't been able to match their former level of success.

Record

World Cup: Winner 1966; fourth place 1990

Olympic Games: Winners 1908, 1912; fourth place 1948

Under-20 World Cup: Fourth place 1981; third place 1993

European Championship: Third place 1968

European Cup: Winners—Manchester United 1968; Liverpool 1977, 1978, 1981, 1984; Nottingham Forest 1979, 1980; Aston Villa 1982

European Cup Winners Cup: Winners—Tottenham Hotspur 1963, West Ham United 1965, Manchester City 1970, Chelsea 1971, Everton 1985, Manchester United 1991

UEFA Cup: Winners—Leeds United 1968, 1971; Newcastle United 1969; Arsenal 1970; Tottenham Hotspur 1972, 1984; Liverpool 1973, 1976; Ipswich Town 1981

Top Players

Gordon Banks Still remembered for his incredible one-handed save from **Pelé** in the 1970 World Cup, this commanding goalie was one of England's heroes four years earlier when the team won the coveted trophy. After his career was cut short by the loss of an eye in a car accident, he courageously returned to play in 1977 and 1978 for Fort Lauderdale in the North American Soccer League.

Bobby Charlton A survivor of the tragic 1958 Munich air crash and younger brother of **Jackie** (the beanpole English center-half who went on to coach Ireland), this elegant inside forward scored a record 49 goals for England in an international career that spanned 106 appearances and included the 1966 World Cup triumph. He also played more than 750 matches for Manchester United, scoring 247 goals and skippering the "Red Devils" to a European Cup win in 1968.

Kevin Keegan This irrepressible midfielder captured English fans' hearts with his nonstop running in more than 60 national team matches. After inspiring Liverpool to a 1977 European Cup title, he moved to West Germany's SV Hamburger and won two European Footballer of the Year awards before returning home to play for Southampton. He later established a successful new career as coach of Newcastle United.

Gary Lineker Top scorer in the 1986 World Cup and one of England's best performers in its great performance four years later, this prolific striker has always had the knack for being in the right place at the right time, although disappointingly, he finished his international career one goal shy of **Bobby Charlton's** record. After helping Barcelona win the 1989 European Cup Winners Cup, he moved back to England with Tottenham Hotspur, then decided to take his waning talents to Nagoya Grampus Eight in Japan's new J League, which started in 1993.

Bobby Moore The most accomplished defender in English history, Moore earned adoration by captaining his team to its sole World Cup victory in 1966. He played 108 games for England and in 1965 led West Ham United to a European Cup Winners Cup title. Moore finished his career in the North American Soccer League, playing for the San Antonio Thunder in 1976 and the Seattle Sounders in 1978. The soccer world was saddened over his premature death from cancer in 1993.

Peter Shilton This stylish and highly reliable goal-keeper followed perfectly in **Gordon Banks'** footsteps by appearing a world-record 125 times in the English jersey and anchoring Nottingham Forest to two successive European Cup wins in 1979 and 1980.

France

Although France played a primary role in the early development and organization of modern soccer, it enjoyed noticeably little success until the 1950s, when the country started to produce its first significant batch of world-class players. The likes of **Just Fontaine** and **Raymond Kopa** helped propel France to a third-place finish in the 1958 World Cup. After another period of relative oblivion, the French bounced back again, producing their best team ever in the 1980s, spearheaded by the magnificent **Michel Platini.** Considered desperately unlucky not to have beaten West Germany in the 1982 World Cup semi-final, France finally realized its huge potential by winning both the European Championship and the Olympic soccer tournament two years later. After another heartbreaking semi-final loss in the 1986 World Cup, French soccer floundered once more, with the failure to qualify for the 1994 tournament a particularly shattering blow. France has achieved little at the club level since Olympique Marseille's historic 1993 European Cup success was quickly tainted by a bribery scandal.

Record

World Cup: Third Place 1958, 1986; fourth place 1982

Olympic Games: Winner 1984; semi-finalists 1908, 1920

In 1982, tiny Liechtenstein, with a total population of 27,000, managed to win 2-0 against China, with a total population of one billion.

European Championship: Winner 1984; fourth place 1960

European Cup: Winner—Olympique Marseille 1993

European Cup Winners Cup: Finalist 1992

UEFA Cup: Finalist 1978

Top Players

Just Fontaine This memorable forward was born in Morocco, but quickly established himself as a prolific goal-scorer in the French league with Reims, reaching his peak during the 1958 World Cup when he scored a record 13 goals for his adopted country. Unfortunately, his budding career was subsequently cut short by two broken legs. He later coached the Moroccan national team.

Raymond Kopa The other half of *le tandem terrible* with **Just Fontaine,** this highly talented forward, famous for his explosive dribbling, was a major reason behind France's third place finish at the 1958 World Cup, although he is also remembered by Spanish fans for helping Real Madrid win three consecutive European Cups between 1957 and 1959 before returning to his beloved Reims.

Jean-Pierre Papin This slightly built striker has quickly become a superstar thanks to his consistent goal-scoring exploits, which won him selection as European Footballer of the Year in 1991, then enabled Olympique Marseille to clinch the European Cup two years later. In 1993, he took his extensive firepower to AC Milan.

Michel Platini Recognized as the greatest French player of all time, this outstanding midfielder became famous for his deadly shooting, especially on direct free kicks, which explains his record 41 goals for the national team in 72 games. Platini twice led France to World Cup semi-finals and in between captained his team to the 1984 European Championship. While at the club level, after 10 seasons with AS Nancy and St. Etienne in the French league, he helped Juventus win both the European Cup Winners Cup in 1984 and the European Cup in 1985. Not surprisingly, he was voted European Footballer of the Year three years in a row from 1983 to 1985.

Germany

The West German national team didn't come into its own until 1954, when it won the first of its three World Cup triumphs. Since then, Germany has become the dominant European country in international competition thanks to a seemingly endless conveyor belt of powerful, talented players supported by first-class coaching. In addition to the country's record six appearances in a World Cup final, Germany has made it through to four European Championship finals, winning two of them. All this success has been achieved with very little assistance from the eastern portion of the country, which competed separately as East Germany from 1948 until reunification in 1990. Only in the Olympic soccer tournament did the pre-reunification East

Germans make their presence felt. The birth of a new professional league, the Bundesliga, in 1963 signaled a dramatic rise in the fortunes of German club soccer, which went through a dominant period during the 1970s when its teams were triumphant in all three major European competitions. The Bundesliga, largely restricted to native-born players, has managed to maintain a consistently high quality of play ever since.

Record

World Cup: Winners 1954, 1974, 1990; finalists 1966, 1982, 1986; third place 1934, 1970; fourth place 1958

Olympic Games: Third place 1988; fourth place 1952 (East Germany: winner 1976, finalist 1980, third place 1964, 1972)

Under-20 World Cup: Winner 1981; finalist 1987 (East Germany: third place 1987)

Under-17 World Cup: Finalist 1985

European Championship: Winners 1972, 1980; finalists 1976, 1992; semi-finalist 1988

European Cup: Winners—Bayern München 1974, 1975, 1976; SV Hamburger 1983

European Cup Winners Cup: Winners—Borussia Dortmund 1966, Bayern München 1967, 1.FC Magdeburg (East Germany) 1974, SV Hamburger 1977, Werder Bremen 1992

UEFA Cup: Winners—Borussia Mönchengladbach 1975, 1979; Eintracht Frankfurt 1980; Bayer Leverkusen 1988

World Club Championship: Winner—Bayern München 1976

Top Players

Franz Beckenbauer "Der Kaiser," as he was deservedly nicknamed, has been at the forefront of German soccer both as a player and a coach for the past 25 years. His silky smooth skills as an archetypal sweeper led Germany to success in the 1972 European Championship and the 1974 World Cup, not to mention one European Cup Winners Cup title in 1967 and three consecutive European Cup victories with Bayern München from 1974 to 1976, as well as two European Footballer of the Year awards in 1972 and 1976. In the twilight of his career, he played for the New York Cosmos from 1977 to 1980, winning three Soccer Bowls, and returned for one more season in 1983 before moving on to coach his beloved Germany. Beckenbauer earned a unique place in the record books by managing the national team to yet another World Cup success in 1990.

Paul Breitner One of the greatest fullbacks of all time, this powerfully built defender became known for his overlapping runs down the flank and even managed to score goals in the World Cup finals of 1974 and 1982. However, he only appeared on one European Cup winning team with Bayern München in 1974, before departing for Real Madrid the following year.

Sepp Maier Yet another member of West Germany's winning World Cup team of 1974, this acrobatic goalkeeper appeared 95 times for his country, also adding a European Championship title (1972), three European Cup titles with Bayern München (1974-76), and one European Cup Winners Cup title with the same club (1967) to his list of honors.

Lothar Matthäus The latest in a long line of phenomenal German superstars, this hugely gifted midfielder drew rave reviews for his performances in leading Germany to success in the 1990 World Cup. After winning the European Footballer of the Year award in 1990, he was recognized the next year as World Footballer of the Year. Most of his career has been spent with Borussia Mönchengladbach and Bayern München, although he had a productive three years with Inter Milan, playing a prime role in its 1991 UEFA Cup win, before joining Bayern München in 1992.

Gerd Müller A natural goal-scorer in every sense of the word, this stockily built striker became a national hero by knocking in the winning goal in the 1974 World Cup final. He went on to score a record 68 goals in just 62 matches for his country and amassed a remarkable 365 goals in the German Bundesliga for Bayern München during a career that featured one European Cup Winners Cup triumph and three European Cup wins. Chosen as European Footballer of the Year in 1970, the same year he scored an unprecedented two hat tricks in the World Cup finals, "Der Bomber" later played in the North American Soccer League for the Fort Lauderdale Strikers from 1979 until 1982.

Karl-Heinz Rummenigge This lanky striker was a standout on West Germany's 1980 European Championship winning side, earning him European Footballer of the Year honors that year and the next. He also appeared on both West German teams that lost World Cup finals in 1982 and 1986. A key player for Bayern München when it won seven Bundesliga titles in the 1980s, he later moved to Inter Milan.

Uwe Seeler Although he represented West Germany in four consecutive World Cup finals from 1958 to 1970, playing a record 21 matches in the process, this short but sturdy center forward, who possessed a wonderful nose for goals, was never able to help his team win the trophy. He spent his entire club career with SV Hamburger, during which he scored more than 550 goals in a little over 700 matches.

Fritz Walter Germany's first true World Cup star led his team to victory in the 1954 tournament, with his creative midfield skills inspiring his teammates to a huge upset of the great Hungarians. His international, as well as club, career was interrupted by World War II.

Holland

One of the first European countries to embrace soccer enthusiastically, Holland reached the semi-finals of the first four Olympic tournaments, although its amateur team could finish no better than third in any of them. The country's soccer program then went into virtual hibernation until it awoke in the 1970s with the advent of a magnificent national team, led by **Johan Cruyff** and coached by **Rinus Michels,** that became famous for its "total soccer" approach of having team members be equally proficient in offense, defense, and midfield skills. Sadly, despite reaching the World Cup final in both 1974 and 1978, the grand trophy itself eluded them. Not until 1988, when a new array of stars had been assembled, was Holland at last able to win a major title, the European Championship. Apart from a memorable period in the 1970s, when the country's three major clubs—Ajax, Feyenoord, and PSV Eindhoven—swept all rivals out of their way in European competition, Dutch league soccer has languished. Most of Holland's major players are now enticed by the bright lights of Italy, Spain, and England.

Record

World Cup: Finalists 1974, 1978

Olympic Games: Third place 1908, 1912; fourth place 1920, 1924

European Championship: Winner 1988; semi-finalist 1992; third place 1976

European Cup: Winners—Feyenoord 1970; Ajax 1971, 1972, 1973; PSV Eindhoven 1988

European Cup Winners Cup: Winner—Ajax 1987

UEFA Cup: Winners—Feyenoord 1974, PSV Eindhoven 1978, Ajax 1992

World Club Championship: Winners—Feyenoord 1970, Ajax 1972

Top Players

Johan Cruyff Arguably the greatest player ever to grace a soccer field other than **Pelé,** this lean but deceptively agile striker electrified Dutch soccer in the early 1970s, during which he single-handedly took Holland to the 1974 World Cup final. A three-time winner of the European Footballer of the Year award (in 1971, 1973, and 1974), he began his career with Ajax Amsterdam, inspiring the team to a hat trick of European Cup wins in 1971, 1972, and 1973, before transferring to Barcelona, then coming out of retirement to play in the North American Soccer League for the Los Angeles Aztecs and the Washington Diplomats from 1979 to 1981. As a coach, he added European Cup Winners Cup titles with Ajax in 1987 and Barcelona in 1989 to his list of achievements. He suffered a mild heart attack, but recovered and went on to mastermind Barcelona's European Cup triumph in 1992.

Ruud Gullit Famous for his dreadlocks and outspoken political views, this free flowing sweeper-turned-midfielder was a shining star for Holland in its 1988 European Championship triumph. Voted European Footballer of the Year in 1987, the same year AC Milan signed him for a record $6 million, he helped his new team to European Cup titles in 1989 and 1990, before moving on to Sampdoria of Italy in

1993. His early Dutch club career included stints with Haarlem, Feyenoord, and PSV Eindhoven.

Rudi Krol A commanding sweeper who looked equally at home whether attacking or defending, this reliable Dutch mainstay appeared in a record 83 matches for his country, including two heartbreaking World Cup final losses in 1974 and 1978 (the latter as captain). He also anchored Ajax's defense for its European Cup wins in 1972 and 1973, later playing briefly for the Vancouver Whitecaps in the North American Soccer League, before Napoli of Italy snapped him up.

Johan Neeskens Yet another member of Holland's "total soccer" World Cup final teams in 1974 and 1978, this handsome midfielder also starred in Ajax's trio of European Cup wins between 1971 and 1973, and, like **Johan Cruyff,** later moved to Barcelona as well as to the United States, where he played for the New York Cosmos from 1979 to 1984, winning two Soccer Bowl titles.

Frank Rijkaard This classy defender-turned-midfielder starred in Holland's 1988 European Championship win and quickly added two European Cup medals with AC Milan in 1989 and 1990. His club career, which began in 1977 with Ajax—for whom he helped win the European Cup Winners Cup in 1987—turned full circle in 1993 when he rejoined his old club.

Marco Van Basten The latest Dutch star to blaze a trail across Europe, this explosive striker spearheaded the team that won the European Championship in 1988. Having already won a European Cup Winners Cup medal with Ajax in 1987, he then joined Gullit and Rijkaard at AC Milan, sparking the team to two successive European Cup victories in 1988 and 1989 and earning himself European Footballer of the Year honors both years (and repeating the feat a third time in 1992, when he reached the highest pinnacle by also being named World Footballer of the Year). A severe leg injury in 1993 threatened to endanger his international career.

Italy

The greatest decade for Italian soccer was probably the 1930s, when the country won two World Cups and an Olympic gold medal under the legendary tutelage of coach **Vittorio Pozzo.** Aside from a period in the 1960s, when Italian teams dominated all three European club competitions and the national team won its only European Championship title, the real glory days did not return until 1982, when Italy secured its third World Cup triumph. This was also the time when the country's Serie A firmly established itself as the best league championship in the world, with a succession of foreign players flocking to Italy in search of fame and fortune. Such superstars as **Michel Platini, Diego Maradona, Ruud Gullit, Marco Van Basten,** and **Lothar Matthäus** have had a stunning impact on Italian club soccer, as evidenced by the country's success in

European competition over the last decade. In 1985, Juventus became the first club to win all three European trophies—a feat only equaled by one other team (Ajax of Holland) to date.

Record

World Cup: Winners 1934, 1938, 1982; finalist 1970; third place 1990; fourth place 1978

Olympic Games: Winner 1936; third place 1928,1960; fourth place 1984, 1988

Under-17 World Cup: Fourth place 1987

European Championship: Winner 1968; semi-finalist 1988; fourth place 1980

European Cup: Winners—AC Milan 1963, 1969, 1989, 1990; Inter Milan 1964, 1965; Juventus 1985

European Cup Winners Cup: Winners—Fiorentina 1961; AC Milan 1968, 1973; Juventus 1984; Sampdoria 1990; Parma 1993

UEFA Cup: Winners—Roma 1961; Juventus 1977, 1990, 1993; Napoli 1989; Inter Milan 1991

World Club Championship: Inter Milan 1964, 1965; AC Milan 1969, 1989, 1990; Juventus 1985

Top Players

Roberto Baggio A superbly talented striker blessed with amazing speed, Baggio achieved a memorable double in 1993 by being selected as both European and World Footballer of the Year. After becoming a huge crowd favorite at Fiorentina, he moved in 1990 to Juventus in a $13 million deal and finally started to repay some of the huge investment by helping his new team win the UEFA Cup in 1993. He played on the Italian team that finished third in the 1990 World Cup.

Franco Baresi One of the most widely respected sweepers ever to play the game, this stalwart defender has become an international fixture, having helped to take his country to the semi-finals of both the 1988 European Championship and the 1990 World Cup. He also anchored the AC Milan defense in its European Cup triumphs of 1989 and 1990.

Giacinto Facchetti This tall, gangly fullback—later converted into a sweeper—who loved to move forward on attack, played 94 times for Italy, leading his country to the European Championship in 1968 and helping it reach the World Cup final two years later. His record 476 appearances for Inter Milan included a remarkable 59 goals and two European Cup trophies in 1964 and 1965.

Gianni Rivera A teen sensation when he made his Italian debut at the tender age of 18, this brilliant midfielder later had his ups and downs with the national team. But his outstanding career with AC Milan, which stretched over 18 years and more than 500 appearances, included two European Cup titles in 1963 and 1969 as well as two European Cup Winners Cup victories in 1968 and 1973.

Paolo Rossi Still chiefly remembered for his dramatic goal-scoring exploits that propelled Italy to an unlikely World Cup win and earned him European Footballer of the Year honors in 1982, this effervescent striker was never able to recapture the form that enabled him to bounce back so dramatically from a two-year suspension for his involvement in a betting scandal. After helping Juventus win the European Cup Winners Cup in 1984 and the European Cup the next year, he was transferred to AC Milan, but further success eluded him.

Dino Zoff Forever famous for captaining Italy to World Cup victory in 1982 at the age of 40, this accomplished goalkeeper had helped his country win the European Championship 14 years earlier. His 114 international matches remain a record, as does his 1,143-minute spell without conceding a goal during the 1972 World Cup. Most of his 570 club matches were played for Juventus (including an incredible 332 in a row at one point), for whom he won a UEFA Cup title in 1977 and later was appointed coach.

Spain

Soccer's early history in Spain is not particularly notable, although in 1929 the national team did become the first country outside the British Isles to defeat England. Then came the Spanish Civil War and World War II to stymie any further progress. Not until the 1950s did Spain really start to stamp its presence on the international soccer field. Clubs in its domestic league began recruiting foreigners to raise the standard of play. Players such as the great **Alfredo Di Stefano** had an immediate effect, for instance, ushering in a remarkable period of ascendancy for Real Madrid both at home and in the European Cup. Later, the two Dutch **Johans—Cruyff** and **Neeskens**—worked similar wonders for Barcelona. But apart from an isolated triumph in the 1964 European Championship, the national team was a major disappointment until it won the 1992 Barcelona Olympic Games.

Record

World Cup: Fourth place 1950

Olympic Games: Winner 1992; third place 1920

Under-20 World Cup: Finalist 1985

Under-17 World Cup: Finalist 1991

European Championship: Winner 1964; finalist 1984

European Cup: Winners—Real Madrid 1956, 1957, 1958, 1959, 1960, 1966; Barcelona 1992

European Cup Winners Cup: Winners—Atlético Madrid 1962; Barcelona 1979, 1982, 1989; Valencia 1980

UEFA Cup: Winners—Barcelona 1958, 1960, 1966; Valencia 1962, 1963; Real Zaragoza 1964; Real Madrid 1985, 1986

World Club Championship: Winners—Real Madrid 1960; Atlético Madrid 1974

Top Players

Emilio Butragueño A real sharpshooter who fully earned his nickname of "El Buitre" (the Vulture), this slender striker won two UEFA Cup titles with Real Madrid in 1985 and 1986. He went on to score four goals for Spain in a remarkable match against Denmark during the 1986 World Cup, finishing his international career with a record 26 goals.

Alfredo Di Stefano Although he made seven appearances for his native Argentina and then played club soccer in Colombia for five years, this truly extraordinary center forward didn't attract world attention until signed by Real Madrid in 1953. The "Blond Arrow of Ríver Plate" went on to score an amazing 405 goals in 624 matches, helping Real Madrid win five European Cup titles, twice being chosen European Footballer of the Year (in 1957 and 1959), and playing 31 international matches (in which he scored 23 goals) as a naturalized Spaniard. He later coached Boca Júniors and Ríver Plate in Argentina and then Valencia and Real Madrid in Spain.

Francisco Gento Famous for his mesmerizing runs down the flank, this speedy winger formed a memorable partnership with **Alfredo Di Stefano,** playing in all eight of the European Cup finals Real Madrid reached between 1956 and 1966 and finishing on the winning team a record six times. He made 43 appearances for Spain without winning any major honors.

Luis Suárez Regarded by many as Spain's greatest native-born player, this elegant inside forward labored for Barcelona in the shadow of the great Real Madrid before being transferred to Inter Milan, where he helped **Helenio Herrera's** famous team capture the European Cup in 1964 and 1965. In 1960, he won European Footballer of the Year honors, and four years later was part of the only Spanish team ever to triumph in the European Championship.

Other Top European Players

George Best (Northern Ireland) A true magician with the ball, this flamboyant winger first came to the fore with Manchester United, scoring in the team's 1968 European Cup triumph and winning the European Footballer of the Year title as a result. However, because of a drinking problem his career then started to crumble. He ended up playing in the North American Soccer League for the Los Angeles Aztecs, the Fort Lauderdale Strikers, and the San Jose Earthquakes.

Jószef Bozsik (Hungary) Famous for his beautifully measured passing, this magnificent midfielder helped Hungary win the 1952 Olympic soccer tournament, but two years later endured supreme disappointment when he was ejected in the infamous "Battle of Berne" World Cup quarter-final against Brazil. His one hundred appearances with the national team remain a Hungarian record.

Kenny Dalglish (Scotland) After a remarkable career with Celtic and then Liverpool, where he won European Cup medals in 1978, 1981, and 1984, this clinically efficient striker, who scored 30 goals during his record 102 appearances for Scotland, became player-coach at Liverpool, achieving considerable success in his new role before abruptly resigning in 1991. He later moved to Blackburn Rovers to concentrate on coaching.

Eusébio (Portugal) Known for his lightning speed and dazzling dribbling skills, this Mozambiquan-born striker scored a record 41 goals for Portugal, the most memorable of which were the four that finally eliminated the upstart North Koreans at the 1966 World Cup. His prolific goal-scoring feats for the Portuguese club Benfica, for whom he helped win a European Cup in 1962, earned him European Footballer of the Year honors in 1965. But in the waning years of his career, he left for the North American Soccer League, where he captained Toronto Metros-Croatia to a championship in 1976 and then played for the Boston Minutemen and the Las Vegas Quicksilvers.

Nandor Hidegkuti (Hungary) A perfect target man, whose main job was to feed the ball to **Ferenc Puskás** and **Sandor Kocsis,** this fine center forward still managed to score 39 goals in 68 international matches. He was a member of Hungary's gold-medal winning Olympic team in 1952 and also played in the 1954 and 1958 World Cups.

Pat Jennings (Northern Ireland) Underneath the quiet, unassuming demeanor of this exceptional goalkeeper lay a steely, determined individual who played more matches (119) for Northern Ireland than anyone else. Most of his career was spent at England's Tottenham Hotspur, where he helped win the UEFA Cup in 1972, although he later played for arch rival Arsenal, too.

Sandor Kocsis (Hungary) Nicknamed "Golden Head" because of his tremendous aerial ability, this superb forward scored a superlative 75 goals, including seven hat tricks (a feat only equaled by **Pelé**), in just 68 matches for Hungary. After winning a gold medal at the 1952 Olympics and fleeing his native country after the 1956 uprising, he joined Barcelona and played on the triumphant UEFA Cup team in 1960.

Denis Law (Scotland) A man with an uncanny knack for finding the net, this bustling forward shares the Scottish goal-scoring record with **Kenny Dalglish,** although he played in half as many matches. Chosen European Footballer of the Year in 1964, he formed a dangerous partnership with **Bobby Charlton** and **George Best** at Manchester United, but, sadly, an injury prevented him from participating in the club's great European Cup success in 1968.

Tottenham Hotspur, one of England's most curiously named teams, owes its unusual moniker to the 15th-century Harry Percy, Duke of Northumberland, popularly known as Hotspur, whose family owned much of what is now the Tottenham district in north London.

Josef Masopust (Czechoslovakia) Unquestionably the greatest Czech ever to play the game, this enterprising midfielder played an integral part in getting his country to the 1962 World Cup final, a performance that was quickly recognized by his selection as European Footballer of the Year. All 17 years of his Czech club career were spent with Dukla Prague.

Ferenc Puskás (Hungary) Although short and somewhat pudgy—hardly the embodiment of a great player—this legendary striker with a famous left-foot rocket-shot terrorized opposing defenses everywhere. He scored a record 83 goals for Hungary in 84 matches, helping his country win the 1952 Olympic soccer title as well as reach the 1954 World Cup final. After the 1956 Hungarian uprising, he began a second career with Real Madrid, where in 372 matches he amassed 324 goals, including a memorable four against Eintracht Frankfurt in the 1960 European Cup final and a hat trick two years later in a losing effort against Portugal's Benfica. He later coached Panathinaikos of Greece to the 1971 European Cup final.

Ian Rush (Wales) Another in a long line of opportunistic British strikers, this slightly built Welshman has scored a host of goals for both club and country. A fixture at Liverpool, apart from one brief foray in Italy, he won a European Cup medal in 1984 and would surely have earned more European trophies had the club not been banned from international competition following the 1985 tragedy at Heysel Stadium in Brussels.

Lev Yashin (Soviet Union) Far and away the most famous player ever to don a Soviet jersey, this magnificent goalkeeper appeared 78 times for his country, helping the team bring home a gold medal at the 1956 Olympic soccer tournament, win the inaugural European Championship in 1960, and reach two quarter-finals and one semi-final of the World Cup. Acclaimed as a Soviet sports hero, he played his entire career for Dynamo Moskva and won the European Footballer of the Year title in 1963.

South America

When soccer's first European missionaries started spreading the gospel at the turn of the century to all the far-flung corners of the world, nobody embraced the message with more fervor than the South Americans. Soccer was actually adopted as the national sport in every single country except Venezuela, where baseball was already king. As early as 1916, the **Confederación Sudamericana de Fútbol**—better known by the equally verbose acronym **CONMEBOL**—was created by Argentina, Uruguay, Brazil, and Chile as the first regional soccer confederation under the FIFA banner. An intense rivalry soon raged between the South Americans and the Europeans, fueled at first by Uruguay's twin successes in the Olympics and historic win in the inaugural World Cup.

This dispute over world soccer supremacy shows no sign of abating. The present World Cup count is delicately balanced at seven wins by South American nations and seven wins by European nations.

CONMEBOL's founding was actually inspired by its four creators' desire to stage a South American championship. The first official tournament in 1916 featured a round-robin league format and the event essentially continued that way until 1975, when the competition was renamed the **Copa América** and restructured to incorporate semi-finals and a final played on a two-leg home-and-away basis (all 10 South American nations competed for the first time). Since 1987, when a single country began hosting the tournament, it has been held every two years. The South American tournament—the world's longest-running soccer championship—has enjoyed a checkered history, partly because it has not always been taken seriously by the likes of Brazil and Argentina. But in 1993, in an effort to revitalize the competition, Mexico and the United States were invited to participate for the first time.

Impressed by the success of the European Cup and wishing to respond to the challenge of a World Club Championship, CONMEBOL launched a club competition of its own in 1960 called the **Copa Libertadores de América**. Since 1966, this colorful tournament has been open to two clubs from each South American nation—both the league champions and the runners-up—with the final always being contested on a home-and-away basis. The Copa Libertadores has suffered its ups and downs, thanks to a series of violent incidents on and off the field as well as several bribery scandals, but it has spawned other club tournaments, including most notably the **Supercopa** for previous winners of the Copa Libertadores.

Argentina

The first country to organize a domestic league in South America, Argentina boasts a long and rich soccer history. As early as 1910, the Argentinian national team won the very first South American championship and quickly established a powerful international reputation, which was reinforced when it reached the final of both the 1928 Olympics and 1930 World Cup, though it was beaten in both by its arch rival Uruguay. Apart from its continuing success in the Copa América, Argentina then retreated into the wilderness for two decades before returning to the international fray in the 1950s, only to find that most of the country's finest players (including the remarkable **Alfredo Di Stefano**) were being filched by Italian clubs. It took two more decades for Argentina to make its presence known in world soccer once more, thanks to two World Cup wins and one appearance in the final—largely inspired by the mercurial **Diego Maradona**. Despite continuing defections across the Atlantic, the Argentinian league remains the strongest on the continent, a fact reflected in the record number of clubs who have triumphed in the Copa Libertadores.

Record

World Cup: Winners 1978, 1986; finalists 1930, 1990

Olympic Games: Finalist 1928

Under-20 World Cup: Winner 1979; finalist 1983

Under-17 World Cup: Third place 1991

Copa América: Winners 1910, 1921, 1925, 1927, 1929, 1937, 1941, 1945, 1946, 1947, 1955, 1957, 1959, 1991, 1993; semi-finalist 1987; third place 1989

Intercontinental Cup: Winner 1992

Copa Libertadores: Winners—Independiente 1964, 1965, 1972, 1973, 1974, 1975, 1984; Rácing Club 1967; Estudiantes 1968, 1969, 1970; Boca Júniors 1977, 1978; Argentinos Júniors 1985; Ríver Plate 1986

Supercopa: Winners—Rácing Club 1988; Boca Júniors 1989

World Club Championship: Rácing Club 1967; Estudiantes 1968; Independiente 1973, 1984; Boca Júniors 1977; Ríver Plate 1986

Top Players

Osvaldo Ardiles Although small, this leanly built midfielder was a surprisingly resilient player who first came to the fore with Argentina's 1978 World Cup winning team. England's Tottenham Hotspur was so impressed that it signed him a month later and he quickly became a fan favorite, helping the team to win the 1984 UEFA Cup. After retiring, he embarked on a coaching career, cutting his teeth with England's West Bromwich Albion and Swindon Town before rejoining Tottenham in 1993.

Mario Kempes Argentina's six-goal hero during its 1978 World Cup win, this elegant striker had made a sufficiently strong impression in the same tournament four years earlier to be signed by Valencia of Spain, for whom he won a European Cup Winners Cup medal in 1980. He was chosen South American Footballer of the Year in 1978.

Diego Maradona One of soccer's all-time greats, this stocky firecracker of a player has had an explosive impact on the sport. After making his debut for Argentina when just 17, he captained his country to victory at the Under-20 World Cup in 1979. Although he disappointed during the 1982 World Cup, he had the tournament of his life four years later when the Argentinians won the coveted trophy. But the moody midfield genius couldn't repeat the feat in 1990, when his repeated conflicts with officials on and off the field interfered with his performance. Maradona began his club career with Argentinos Júniors and Boca Júniors and was recognized as South American Footballer of the Year in 1979 and 1980. He was transferred to Barcelona of Spain in 1982, but two relatively unproductive years later he was on the move again to Napoli of Italy, where in 1989 he helped his new team win the UEFA Cup. In 1991, he was forced to leave Napoli in disgrace after testing positive for cocaine and receiving a 15-month worldwide ban. Finally, after a

brief spell with Sevilla of Spain, he returned to Argentina to play for Newell's Old Boys.

Omar Sivori Noted for his thrilling ball skills as well as his notorious temper (he holds the record for ejections), this skillful forward began his career at Ríver Plate and appeared 12 times for Argentina, including its 1957 Copa América win, before moving across the Atlantic for a world-record transfer fee to play for Juventus, where he formed a lethal striking partnership with Welshman **John Charles.** He won the European Footballer of the Year Award in 1961 and also made nine international appearances for his newly adopted Italy.

Brazil

The first country to win three World Cups, Brazil is still regarded by many as the premier soccer nation. But the development of a strong national team took many years, and not until the 1950s did Brazil achieve any real measure of success. At that point, only three South American championships had been secured, each on home soil, and the country didn't even enter the Olympic soccer tournament until 1952. After a huge upset loss to Uruguay in the 1950 World Cup final and another disappointment four years later, Brazil's dazzling artistry was finally rewarded with a much-deserved triumph in 1958, the World Cup that marked **Pelé's** debut. Essentially the same team emerged victorious again in 1962, but it was the 1970 winning team that drew applause and envy from the rest of the world. Since then, the ghosts of these past teams have come to haunt Brazilian soccer, and despite appearing in World Cup semi-finals in 1974 and 1978 and reaching Olympic finals in 1984 and 1988, the country has had little to show for itself—just one more Copa América title, for instance. In the absence of a nationwide league, Brazilian club soccer—organized instead on a state-by-state basis—has been surprisingly weak, as its poor Copa Libertadores record demonstrates.

Record

World Cup: Winners 1958, 1962, 1970; finalist 1950; third place 1938, 1978; fourth place 1974

Olympic Games: Finalists 1984, 1988; fourth place 1976

Under-20 World Cup: Winners 1983, 1985, 1993; finalist 1991; third place 1977, 1989

Under-17 World Cup: Third place 1985

Copa América: Winners 1919, 1922, 1949, 1989; semi-finalists 1975, 1979

Copa Libertadores: Winners—Santos 1962, 1963; Cruzeiro 1976; Flamengo 1981; Gremio 1983; São Paulo 1992, 1993

Supercopa: Winner—Cruzeiro 1991, 1992; São Paulo 1993

World Club Championship: Santos 1962, 1963; Flamengo 1981; Gremio 1983; São Paulo 1992, 1993

Top Players

Didi (Waldir Pereira) A midfield maestro famous for his viciously curving banana kicks, Didi orchestrated Brazil's magnificent march to victory at the 1958 World Cup and followed this up four years later with another series of masterful performances as Brazil triumphed once again. Most of his club career was spent with Fluminense and Botafogo, although he did have one unhappy season with Real Madrid in 1960 before returning to his native Brazil. In 1970, he coached a fine Peruvian national team to the quarter-finals of the World Cup.

Garrincha (Manuel Francisco dos Santos) Despite a debilitating bout with polio as a child, which left one of his legs somewhat bowed, this glorious winger became one of the greatest dribblers in soccer history. His mesmerizing runs were a dominant factor in Brazil's two consecutive World Cup triumphs in 1958 and 1962. From 1953 to 1966, he played for Botafogo, but injuries, marital problems, and alcoholism finally ended his career and later contributed to his untimely death at the age of 49 in 1983.

Jairzinho (Jair Ventura Filho) The natural successor to **Garrincha,** this devastating winger with his incomparable rocket-shot catapulted to fame at the 1970 World Cup by becoming only the second player to score in every match during a finals tournament. He became almost a lone star for Brazil at the 1974 World Cup, finishing his international

Soccer Tragedies

Over the years soccer seems to have suffered more than its fair share of natural disasters and other tragic events:

1902 Stand collapses at Glasgow's Ibrox Park during a Scotland vs. England match, killing 25 and injuring 517.

1946 A wall breaks at Burnden Park, Bolton, before start of an English Football Association Cup match between Bolton Wanderers and Stoke City, killing 33 and injuring more than 400.

1949 A plane crashes into Superga Basilica, killing the entire Torino team (and many officials) just days before the club was expected to win its fifth consecutive Italian championship.

1958 A plane crashes at Munich Airport, killing eight players, the coach, and two other club officials of Manchester United (as well as eight journalists) after the club had just reached the European Cup semi-final.

1962 A landslide hits a stadium in Libreville during a match between Gabon and Congo-Brazzaville, killing nine and injuring 30.

1964 A riot breaks out near the end of the Olympic qualifying match in Lima, with Argentina leading Peru 1-0, when a referee disallows a Peruvian goal; the disturbance quickly spreads from the stadium into the city center, leaving 301 dead and more than 500 injured.

1968 Celebrations by River Plate fans at Estadio Monumental, Buenos Aires, after a match with Boca Júniors create a stampede, killing 74 and injuring more than 150.

1969 A plane crashes in the Andes, killing the entire team and all club officials of The Strongest, a top Bolivian team.

1971 A barrier collapses at Ibrox Park, Glasgow, minutes before the end of a Rangers vs. Celtic match, killing 66 and injuring more than 140.

1977 A Colombian second division match is halted when Santa Rosa de Cabal replacement goalkeeper Libardo Zuniga is kicked in the groin by an opposing striker and dies.

Celebrations in São Paulo, Brazil, after Corinthians Paulista wins the São Paulo league title, leave 15 dead.

1979 A plane crashes during a flight in the Soviet Union, killing 17 team members of Pakhtator Tashkent.

1982 Icy conditions and locked exits at Lenin Stadium, Moscow, create a major crush at the end of a UEFA Cup match between Spartak Moscow and Haarlem of Holland, killing 69, according to official Soviet accounts. Later investigations suggest that 340 died, making it the worst soccer disaster ever.

1985 English fans riot before the start of the European Cup final between Liverpool and Juventus, causing a wall to collapse at Heysel Stadium, Brussels, killing 39 and injuring 454. As a result, 14 Liverpool fans receive prison sentences and FIFA bans English clubs from all European cup competitions.

A stand at Valley Parade Stadium, Bradford, burns down during an English third division match between Bradford City and Lincoln City, killing 55 and injuring 210.

1987 A plane crashes in Peru, killing the entire team and all club officials of Alianza Lima.

1988 A hailstorm in Katmandu, Nepal, during a match between Nepal and Bangladesh causes a stampede, killing 71.

1989 Overcrowding at Hillsborough Stadium, Sheffield, England, before the start of the Football Association Cup semi-final between Liverpool and Nottingham Forest creates a major crush, killing 95 and injuring 170.

1991 Post-match "celebrations" in Santiago after Chilean champions Colo Colo beat Olimpia of Paraguay 3-0 in the Libertadores Cup leave 10 dead, 135 injured, and 188 under arrest.

1992 A portable stand collapses at Furiani Stadium, Corsica, just before the start of the French Cup semi-final between Bastia and Marseilles, killing 13 and injuring nearly 700.

1993 A plane crashes off the Gabon coast, killing 18 players and five club officials of the Zambian national team on its way to play a World Cup qualifying match in Senegal.

career with 38 goals in 87 matches. After spending most of his career at Botafogo, a brief interlude followed at Olympique Marseille in France before he returned to his native Brazil to play for Cruzeiro, where he won a Copa Libertadores medal in 1976.

Leônidas (Leônidas da Silva) Nicknamed *O Diamante Negro* (the Black Diamond) and *O Homen Borracha* (the Rubber Man) and famous for popularizing the bicycle kick, this supremely agile center forward made his debut at the age of 19 for Brazil in 1932, played in the 1934 World Cup, and established himself as a major international star four years later with several breathtaking World Cup performances, including a four-goal performance against Poland. His Brazilian club affiliations included Vasco da Gama, Botafogo, Flamengo, and São Paulo, but wherever he played, success followed him.

Pelé (Edson Arantes do Nascimento) Not just the most famous player in soccer history but also unquestionably the best, this almost mythical figure has become an icon of the sport, revered almost as much in the United States as he is in his native Brazil. He became an international star at the age of 17 with his incredible two-goal performance against Sweden in the 1958 World Cup final. Although he missed most of the 1962 tournament because of injury and in the 1966 finals defenders from competing teams viciously kicked him to such an extent that he had to leave the tournament prematurely with painful injuries, he returned to glory with a stupendous display in the 1970 World Cup, scoring a brilliant header in the final against Italy to win the trophy. Nicknamed *Pérola Negra* (Black Pearl), Pelé played all his club soccer for Santos. Officially declared a national treasure by the Brazilian Congress in 1960 to ensure he couldn't be poached away by any European teams, Pelé won Copa Libertadores honors for his team in 1962 and 1963, landed the South American Footballer of the Year title in 1973, and didn't retire until 1974, by which time he had scored 1,280 goals, including a record 97 in international matches and an incredible 92 hat tricks. In 1975, he created a sensation by coming out of retirement to take on the messianic role of playing for the New York Cosmos in the North American Soccer League, subsequently leading his new team to the Soccer Bowl title in 1977, the year he bade farewell to soccer for the second and final time.

Tostão (Eduardo Gonçalves de Andrade) One of the unsung heroes of Brazilian soccer, it was Tostão's unselfish brilliance as a pivotal center forward that laid the way for Brazil to win the 1970 World Cup. He made his international debut at the age of 19, appearing a few months later in the 1966 World Cup, but a serious eye injury in 1969 appeared to have ended his career. In characteristic fashion, though, he bounced right back to confound the soccer world in 1970. From 1963 to 1972, he achieved great success with Cruzeiro, was chosen South American Footballer of the Year in 1971, and then ended his playing days at Vasco da Gama.

Zico (Artur Antunes Coimbra) Christened the "White Pelé," this superb attacking midfielder never quite lived up to his billing, although after getting very little playing time in the 1978 World Cup, he made a much more dynamic contribution four years later, only to endure heartbreak at the 1986 tournament by missing a vital penalty kick in the quarter-finals against France. Second only to Pelé, he scored 54 goals for Brazil in 78 games. Apart from two unhappy seasons with Udinese in Italy, his entire career was spent with Flamengo, for whom he scored more than 500 goals, playing on the team that won the 1981 Libertadores Cup and winning South American Footballer of the Year honors in 1977, 1981, and 1982. After retiring, he became his country's sports minister, but then in 1991 attempted a comeback by playing in the Japanese league.

Uruguay

Many soccer observers believe Uruguayan soccer continues to rest on the laurels of its past. Certainly, few countries can match the startling run of success that Uruguay achieved earlier this century with gold medal wins in the 1924 and 1928 Olympics, four Copa América triumphs between 1920 and 1926, and a sweet victory in 1930 at the inaugural World Cup. Then the national team all but dropped out of international sight, only surfacing again in 1950 to defeat a heavily favored Brazil and to celebrate its second World Cup title. Uruguay came close to winning a third World Cup in 1954 and 1970, but in the last few decades, international success has largely deserted the team—other than back-to-back Copa América titles in 1983 and 1987. On the domestic front, the Uruguayan league has been dominated by Peñarol and Nacional. In fact, between 1932 and 1983, only one other team managed to break the stranglehold these two clubs had on the championship. Peñarol and Nacional have managed to reproduce this success in the Copa Libertadores, winning more titles than any other team except Independiente of Argentina.

Record

World Cup: Winners 1930, 1950; fourth place 1954, 1970

Olympic Games: Winners 1924, 1928

Under-20 World Cup: Third place 1979; fourth place 1977

Copa América: Winners 1916, 1917, 1920, 1923, 1924, 1926, 1935, 1942, 1956, 1959, 1967, 1983, 1989; semi-finalist 1975; third place 1989

Copa Libertadores: Winners—Peñarol 1960, 1961, 1966, 1982, 1987; Nacional 1971, 1980, 1988

World Club Championship: Winners—Peñarol 1961, 1966, 1982; Nacional 1971, 1980, 1988

Top Players

Jose Leandro Andrade Still a legend in Uruguayan soccer, this exceptionally skillful halfback inspired his country to gold medal wins in the 1924 and 1928 Olympic Games and then came out of retirement two years later to play an instrumental role in Uruguay's victory at the inaugural World Cup. He also helped the national team win Copa América titles in 1923, 1924, and 1926 and achieved great success with his club team, Nacional.

Enzo Francescoli This flamboyant striker has had something of an international roller-coaster ride, having shone during the 1986 World Cup only to be a major disappointment in the same tournament four years later. He helped Uruguay win the Copa América in 1983, a feat the team repeated in 1987, and was hailed as South American Footballer of the Year in 1984. After an illustrious early career with Ríver Plate of Argentina, he tried his hand in Europe, playing for Racing Club de Paris and Olympique Marseille in France before moving on to Cagliari and Torino in Italy.

Juan Schiaffino A diminutive figure on the soccer field, this frail-looking forward was nevertheless a force to be reckoned with who earned his country's everlasting adulation by engineering a monumental upset in the 1950 World Cup final against Brazil. His finest match was probably the epic semi-final encounter four years later when Hungary prevailed only after he was forced to leave the match injured. After great success in the Uruguayan league with Peñarol, a transfer fee that set a world record in 1954 enticed him away to AC Milan, where he became a star player before ending his career with Roma.

Obdulio Varela Captain of the Uruguayan team that shocked everyone in 1950 by beating heavily favored Brazil to win the World Cup, this resolute central defender provided a firm anchor throughout the tournament and might have repeated the feat four years later had he not been injured and unable to play in the key semi-final match against Hungary. He also captained his club team, Peñarol, with great success.

Other Top South American Players

Teofilo Cubillas (Peru) One of South America's most attractive players, this brilliant attacking midfielder, famed for his fierce shooting ability, single-handedly took Peru to the quarter-finals of the 1970 World Cup at the tender age of 20, scoring a remarkable five goals in the process. In 1972, success with the national team as well as club team Alianza Lima led to his selection as South American Footballer of the Year, and three years later he inspired his country to a memorable Copa América triumph. In 1973, he was transferred to FC Basel in Switzerland and then to FC Porto in Portugal, but he returned to the international limelight by scoring another five goals for Peru in the 1978 World Cup, which in turn precipitated a move to the Fort Lauderdale Strikers of the North American Soccer League, where he played for five seasons.

Elias Figueroa (Chile) This talented sweeper appeared in the 1966 and 1974 World Cups for Chile, but it was his standout play for the Brazilian club team Internacional Porto Alegre that earned him the title of South American Footballer of the Year three times in a row from 1974 to 1976. After helping his country to reach the final of the Copa América in 1979, he closed out his career by playing the 1981 season for the Fort Lauderdale Strikers of the North American Soccer League.

Julio Cesar Romero (Paraguay) The finest player ever to appear for Paraguay, this industrious midfielder was the creative genius behind his country's remarkable success in the 1979 Copa América, then performed more miracles to help take the team into the second round of the 1986 World Cup. In 1980, he joined the New York Cosmos of the North American Soccer League for three seasons, helping to win two Soccer Bowl titles before moving to Fluminense of Brazil. He was voted South American Footballer of the Year in 1985.

Carlos Valderrama (Colombia) Almost as famous for his immense mane of shaggy hair as for his performances on a soccer field, this exciting midfielder was inspirational in getting Colombia into the semi-finals of the Copa América in 1987, earning himself South American Footballer of the Year honors in the process. Three years later, he helped his country reach the second round of the World Cup for the first time in its history. Most of his club career has been spent in Europe with Montpelier of France and Real Valladolid of Spain.

Central America and the Caribbean

With the exception of Mexico, soccer has never captured the attention of the Central American and Caribbean nations in the way it has their neighbors to the south. Rival sports such as baseball and cricket hold far greater sway in some countries, while continuing political turmoil has retarded soccer's development in others. Mexico, a hotbed of soccer from the early years of this century, gained its FIFA affiliation in 1929 and was then content to go it alone. Not surprisingly, attempts to cobble together a confederation from the other nations in the region went nowhere until the **Confederación Centroamericana y del Caribe de Fútbol (CCCF)** came into being in 1938. Mexico flirted with a **North American Football Confederation** the following year, which quickly collapsed. Finally, in 1961, Mexico realized that if international soccer was ever to flourish in the region, a strong confederation was essential—and so was born the **Confederación Norte-Centroamericana y del Fútbol,** with its equally daunting acronym **CONCACAF**.

A CONCACAF Championship has been held since 1941, but not until 50 years later, when the United States, participating for the first time, stage-managed the entire proceedings and rechristened it the **Gold Cup,** did the competition finally achieve the stature it deserved. Qualification tournaments were held in both the Caribbean and Central America. However, the **CONCACAF Champions Cup** for the region's top club teams—first held in 1962 and completely dominated by the Mexicans—still has a long way to go, although recent sponsorship assistance from American Airlines and renewed interest from U.S. teams promises much for the future.

Mexico

Until the recent improvement in the standard of both American and Canadian play, Mexico was the sole powerhouse in the CONCACAF region. Mexican soccer has a long and distinguished history, stretching back to 1903, when the Mexican league championship began. However, the national team didn't make its initial appearance until 1928 at the Amsterdam Olympics. Two years later, Mexico competed in the inaugural World Cup, and although the team has never made it past the quarter-finals in this and eight subsequent tournaments, the country has hosted soccer's premier event twice, an honor only equaled by Italy. In recent years, the national team has performed better than ever before, as shown by Mexico's stunning achievement in reaching the 1993 Copa América final at its first attempt. The following month, the Mexicans wrapped up their fourth CONCACAF Championship. Domestic league play has improved considerably in the past few years and now boasts an American-style alignment of four divisions with four teams each. Not surprisingly, Mexican teams have reigned supreme in the CONCACAF Champions Cup.

Record

World Cup: Never gone beyond quarter-finals

Olympic Games: Fourth place 1968

Under-20 World Cup: Finalist 1977

CONCACAF Championship (Gold Cup): Winners 1965, 1971, 1977, 1993

Copa América: Finalist 1993

CONCACAF Champions Cup: Winners—Club Deportivo Guadalajara 1962; Toluca 1968; Cruz Azul 1969, 1970, 1971; Atlético Español 1975; Club América 1977, 1987, 1990, 1992; Universidad Autónoma Guadalajara 1978; Universidad Nacional Autónoma de Mexico 1980, 1982, 1989; Atlante 1983; Puebla 1991

Top Players

Antonio Carbajal A resilient goalkeeper with a remarkable record of longevity, he is the only player to have played in five World Cup finals, having kept goal in the 1950, 1954, 1958, 1962, and 1966 tournaments.

Hugo Sanchez A major reason for Mexico's extraordinary showing in the 1986 World Cup, when it would have reached the semi-finals but for a penalty shootout loss to West Germany, this

dangerous striker began his career with Universidad Nacional Autónoma de Mexico, simultaneously playing two seasons for the San Diego Sockers of the North American Soccer League before parading his talents in Europe, first for Atlético Madrid and then for Real Madrid, where he helped win the UEFA Cup in 1986. In 1992, he returned to his homeland to play for Club América but came back to Spain the following season to play for Rayo Vallecano.

Africa

For the first half of this century in Africa, the development of soccer, just like that of political self-determination, was held back by European colonialism. When Egypt, Ethiopia, South Africa, and Sudan eventually banded together to form the **Confédération Africaine de Football (CAF)** in 1957, this body became the first major organization of any kind ever created by independent African countries. The CAF is now the largest confederation within FIFA, boasting 50 member nations, and with the surging growth and success of African soccer—it's the premier sport in almost every country—have come loud calls for greater representation in the World Cup finals. In 1982, Africa's allocation of qualifying countries doubled from one to two, then increased to three for the 1994 tournament in the United States, but many believe this is still not a fair representation of the continent's strength.

No sooner had the CAF come into being than the first **African Nations Cup** was kicked off, albeit without South Africa, whose all-white delegation had been promptly expelled. From the tournament's humble beginnings, a powerful single-elimination championship has evolved, held every two years in a different country and preceded by a sophisticated qualifying tournament. In 1964, the **African Cup of Champion Clubs** made its debut, with the winning club in each member country's league competition eligible to enter. Eleven years later came the **African Cup Winners Cup** for the winner of each country's single-elimination competition. In both competitions, single-elimination matches culminate in a home-and-away final decided by aggregate score.

Former England coach Graham Taylor regularly invoked the ire of the British press for a string of losses that culminated in the country's failure to qualify for the 1994 World Cup finals. A particularly uninspiring defeat against Sweden in the 1992 European Championship provoked a classic headline in the *Sun* newspaper: "Swedes 2 Turnips 1," accompanied by a picture of a turnip superimposed on Taylor's head. When England was severely beaten by Norway in a World Cup qualifying match, one newspaper came up with "Norse Manure," while another pronounced "End of the World." But a 2-0 loss to the United States proved to be the final straw. "Wanted Dead or Alive—Outlaw of English Football," thundered the *Sun*.

Algeria

Since gaining independence from France in 1962, Algeria has achieved a considerable amount of success on the soccer field, especially during the 1980s when the national team appeared in two consecutive World Cups. In the first round of the 1982 tournament, Algeria pulled off perhaps the greatest victory ever by an African nation—an amazing 2-1 upset of West Germany. Incredibly, the team went on to beat Chile, too, and only failed to move on to the next round because of a West German win. In recent years, Algeria has been very competitive in the African Nations Cup and finally won the tournament in 1990. In spite of regional politics and other diversions, Algerian clubs have also performed creditably in the African Cup, with three teams having emerged victorious.

Record

World Cup: Never gone beyond first round

Olympic Games: Never gone beyond quarter-finals

African Nations Cup: Winner 1990; finalist 1980; third place 1984; fourth place 1982, 1988

African Cup of Champion Clubs: Winners—MC Algiers 1976; JS Kabylie 1981, 1990; ES Setif 1988

African Cup Winners Cup: Finalist 1978

Top Players

Lakhdar Belloumi Voted African Footballer of the Year in 1981, this great midfielder was the inspiration behind Algeria's performance at the 1982 and 1986 World Cups. Unlike many of his compatriots, he was never tempted away to Europe, playing his entire club career for GC Mascara.

Rabah Madjer Another hero from 1982 and 1986, this accomplished striker made headlines in 1987 by scoring the first goal in an historic European Cup win by FC Porto of Portugal, an achievement that deservedly won him African Footballer of the Year honors.

Cameroon

No African nation has progressed farther in the World Cup than the "Indomitable Lions" of Cameroon, who reached the quarter-finals of the 1990 tournament and would have made it through to the semi-finals had the team not conceded two penalties against England. Cameroon first came into the international limelight in the 1980s by battling its way to three consecutive African Nations Cup finals, two of which the country managed to win. The success of the national team has been built on the strength of the country's club league, dominated by Canon Yaoundé, Tonnerre Yaoundé, and Union Douala. These three clubs have also made a big impact in Africa's two major club competitions, having won seven titles among them. In recent years, though, the well seems to have run dry: the last victory occurred in 1981.

Record

World Cup: Never gone beyond quarter-finals

Olympic Games: Never gone beyond second round

African Nations Cup: Winners 1984, 1988; finalist 1986; third place 1972; fourth place 1992

African Cup of Champion Clubs: Winners—Oryx Douala 1964; Canon Yaoundé 1971, 1978, 1980; Union Douala 1979

African Cup Winners Cup: Tonnerre Yaoundé 1975; Canon Yaoundé 1979; Union Douala 1981

Top Players

Roger Milla Brought out of semi-retirement on the island of Réunion, this extraordinary striker proved to be a revelation in the 1990 World Cup, scoring four goals, stretching opposing defenses to the very limit. Not surprisingly, he was soon after recognized as African Footballer of the Year. A member of the Cameroon team that won the African Nations Cup in 1984 and 1988, he also played on the 1982 World Cup team. After beginning his career at Canon Yaoundé, he was transferred to Montpelier in France. He finally hung up his boots at the conclusion of the 1990 World Cup and became coach of Tonnerre Yaoundé and then technical director of the national team.

Thomas N'Kono Cameroon's towering goalkeeper made a lasting impression at the 1982 World Cup, in which he conceded only one goal, and was also between the nets eight years later for his country's even more stunning achievement in reaching the quarter-finals. Twice elected African Footballer of the Year (in 1979 and 1982), he played for Canon Yaoundé until his transfer to Español of Spain in 1982.

Egypt

Having joined FIFA way back in 1923, Egypt continues to enjoy its role as the elder statesman of African soccer. A domestic cup competition was introduced in 1922, by far the earliest competition of its kind on the continent, and a national league followed in 1949. Cairo's top two clubs, Al Ahly and Zamalek, have achieved complete ascendancy over both competitions, having won all but six league titles. The "derby" match between these two ferocious rivals is guaranteed to draw a crowd of 100,000 to the International Stadium. Al Ahly and Zamalek have also made their presence felt throughout the continent by winning five African Cups and four African Cup Winners Cups. Similar success has largely eluded Egypt's national team, however, with only three African Nations Cup wins (two of which date back to the late 1950s), a couple of semi-final appearances in the Olympic tournament, and two somewhat uninspiring first round performances in the World Cup to show for itself.

Record

World Cup: Never gone beyond first round

Olympic Games: Fourth place 1928, 1964

African Nations Cup: Winners 1957, 1959, 1986; finalist 1962; third place 1963, 1970, 1974; fourth place 1976, 1980, 1984

African Cup of Champion Clubs: Winners—Ismaili 1969; Al Ahly 1982, 1987; Zamalek 1984, 1986, 1993

African Cup Winners Cup: Winners—Arab Contractors 1982, 1983; Al Ahly 1984, 1985, 1986, 1993

Top Player

Mahmoud Al Khatib The greatest forward ever to play for Egypt ended his career on an appropriate note by leading his country to victory in the 1986 African Nations Cup. A stalwart with Al Ahly, he was selected African Footballer of the Year in 1983.

Ghana

Even before Ghana gained independence in 1957, soccer was well established there, with a profusion of regional tournaments held on a regular basis throughout the country. In 1958, Ghana had the distinction of being the first sub-Saharan African nation to join FIFA and quickly developed a national team that became the envy of the entire continent by winning the 1963 and 1965 African Nations Cups and reaching the finals of the next two tournaments, as well as making a quarter-final appearance in the 1964 Olympics. Two more Nations Cup wins followed in 1978 and 1982, giving the country an unprecedented four titles, and another victory was only prevented in 1992 when Ghana lost 11-10 on penalty kicks to Côte d'Ivoire. Yet the national team has never managed to get past the qualifying rounds in the World Cup, although it did win its first world title by triumphing at the Under-17 level in 1991 and almost duplicated this success in the Under-20 tournament two years later. In between, it reached the semi-final of the 1992 Olympics with its Under-23 team. At the club level, Asante Kotoko has dominated the Ghanaian league, having managed to win two African Cup titles in the process.

Record

World Cup: Never qualified for finals

Olympic Games: Third place 1992

Under-20 World Cup: Finalist 1993

Under-17 World Cup: Winner 1991; finalist 1993

African Nations Cup: Winners 1963, 1965, 1978, 1982; finalists 1968, 1970, 1992

African Cup of Champion Clubs: Winners—Asante Kotoko 1970, 1983

African Cup Winners Cup: No club has ever gone beyond semi-finals

Top Players

Abedi Pelé A runaway choice as African Footballer of the Year in 1991, this superb striker achieved worldwide recognition two years later with his stellar performance for Olympique Marseille in the European Cup final. His goals helped Ghana reach the 1992 African Nations Cup final, but his absence in the vital match through injury proved crucial as Côte d'Ivoire won on penalties.

Nii Lamptey A rapidly rising star who first came to the fore as a 14-year-old at the 1989 Under-17 World Cup, and subsequently played a starring role two years later during Ghana's triumph in the same tournament, this engaging striker also made his presence felt at the African Nations Cup the following year and at the Under-20 World Cup in 1993. He also opened many eyes while playing for RSC Anderlecht of Belgium.

Morocco

Home to the oldest domestic league in Africa, Morocco also boasts one of the best organized and most diverse club competitions on the continent. Such is the strength of the country's soccer infrastructure—stadiums, communications, transportation, and so on—that Morocco put in a strong bid to host the 1994 World Cup, but ultimately lost out to the United States. Until 1994, the national team had qualified for the world's premier event twice, impressing many with a workmanlike performance in 1970 and then positively shocking the soccer experts in 1986 by besting England, Poland, and Portugal to win its first-round group before narrowly losing to West Germany in the next round. Little success has been achieved in Olympic soccer tournaments, however, and Morocco's record in the African Nations Cup is surprisingly spotty, with just one win under its belt. Only twice have Moroccan teams triumphed in the two major African club competitions.

Record

World Cup: Never gone beyond second round

Olympic Games: Never gone beyond second round

African Nations Cup: Winner 1976; third place 1980, 1988; fourth place 1986

African Cup of Champion Clubs: Winners—FAR Rabat 1985; Raja Casablanca 1989

African Cup Winners Cup: No club has ever gone beyond quarter-finals

Soccer has a long history of using nicknames, but the most colorful are those of Africa's various national teams: the Indomitable Lions of Cameroon, the Leopards of Zaire, the Green Eagles of Nigeria, the Black Stars of Ghana, the Elephants of Ivory Coast, the Stallions of Upper Volta, the Cranes of Uganda, and the KK Eleven (named after former president Kenneth Kaunda) of Zambia. Even individual players have special sobriquets: Egypt's Hossam Hassan is known as "The Diamond of the Pyramids," while his teammate Taher Abu Zeid is called "The Maradona of the Nile."

Top Players

Badou Zaki One of the main reasons for Morocco's extraordinary performance in the 1986 World Cup, this outstanding goalkeeper only gave up two goals in four matches and was suitably rewarded by being selected African Footballer of the Year several months later.

Aziz Bouderbala Another prominent member of the 1986 World Cup team, he subsequently went on to make quite a name for himself with various French clubs, including Racing Club de Paris and Olympique Lyonnais.

Nigeria

Despite its prominence as Africa's most populous and oil-rich nation, Nigeria has had to endure a long slog to establish its soccer credentials. Not until 1976 did the national team even manage to qualify for the African Nations Cup, but just four years later it won the prestigious trophy. Since then, Nigeria has made it through to three finals, although each time it has come away empty-handed. World Cup qualification proved equally elusive until 1994, and only twice has a Nigerian team participated in an Olympic soccer tournament, falling at the first hurdle each time. However, this relative international drought was dramatically shattered in 1985 with Nigeria's stunning success in the Under-17 World Cup, the first world title for an African country. Proving that this was no fluke, the country repeated the feat eight years later and also managed to reach the final of the Under-20 World Cup in between. On the domestic front, Nigeria is unusual in that its single-elimination tournament enjoys more prestige than its league counterpart.

Record

World Cup: Never qualified for finals until 1994

Olympic Games: Never gone beyond first round

Under-20 World Cup: Finalist 1989; third place 1985

Under-17 World Cup: Winner 1985, 1993; finalist 1987

African Nations Cup: Winner 1980; finalists 1984, 1988, 1990; third place 1976, 1978, 1992

African Cup of Champion Clubs: Finalists: 1975, 1984, 1988

African Cup Winners Cup: Winners—IICC Shooting Stars 1976; Enugu Rangers 1977; BCC Lions 1990

Top Player

Stephen Keshi A resolute veteran defender who endeared himself to all of Nigeria by leading his team to qualification for the 1994 World Cup, Keshi played on both the 1984 and 1988 teams that reached the final of the African Nations Cup. After beginning his club career with New Nigerian Bank, he moved to Europe to play for RSC Anderlecht (appearing in the 1990 European Cup Winners Cup) and Molenbeek of Belgium, before being transferred to Racing Club de Strasbourg of France.

Asia

Although soccer was exported to most Asian nations by the European colonial powers around the turn of the last century, the game made little headway until after World War II. In 1951, the Asian Games introduced a soccer tournament, but the most significant event occurred three years later when 13 countries formed the fledgling **Asian Football Confederation (AFC)** and decided to organize their own international championship. The first **Asian Cup** took place in 1956 and has been held every four years since. Initially decided on a league basis, it now begins with a qualifying tournament, from which round-robin play leads to semi-finals and a final.

Asian club soccer has yet to catch on. An **Asian Champion Teams' Cup** has been played intermittently, and more recently an **Asian Cup Winners Cup** was also introduced, but the continent is so vast that many teams are not prepared to travel the huge distances necessary. Many countries are concentrating instead on their own domestic competition. South Korea, for instance, instigated a professional league in 1983, and Japan launched its heavily sponsored J League with much fanfare in 1993.

However, soccer continues to languish in some very populous parts of the continent. In India, for instance, the sport has been largely elbowed aside by cricket and field hockey, while China has shown little serious interest in soccer.

Iran

With more than 6,000 clubs and over 300,000 officially registered players, Iran has remained a hotbed of soccer despite the Islamic Revolution in 1979, after which the Ayatollah Khomeini inexplicably banned the sport for a short time. But it was the Shah of Iran, by encouraging the employment of top foreign coaches, who put Iran on the international soccer map in the 1960s and 1970s.

From 1968 to 1976, the national team won three consecutive Asian Cups without losing a single match, reached the quarter-finals of the 1976 Olympics, and qualified for the 1978 World Cup finals for the first time in its history. The result was a predictable first round exit, but not before it had tied Scotland 1-1. Since then, Iran has achieved three third-place Asian Cup finishes in a row.

Kuwait won the 1990 Gulf Cup just before the Iraqi invasion of 2 August. During the ensuing war the Cup itself disappeared, allegedly stolen by Iraq. It turned up in, of all places, a small trophy store in Ely, England.

Record

World Cup: Never gone beyond first round

Olympic Games: Never gone beyond quarter-finals

Asian Cup: Winners 1968, 1972, 1976; third place 1980, 1984, 1988

Saudi Arabia

Until Saudi Arabia started to use its oil resources to build huge stadiums and to attract some of the world's top coaches, soccer had very little foothold in this large Arab nation. But in the 1980s, the vast infusion of oil money started to reap dividends when the national team walked away with two impressive victories in the Asian Cup. Saudi Arabia almost made it three in a row by reaching the 1992 final, but this time Japan emerged triumphant on its home soil—just one week before, the Saudis had gained even more respect by reaching the final of the first ever Intercontinental Cup, losing to Argentina but finishing ahead of the United States and Côte d'Ivoire. However, only once have the Saudis appeared in an Olympic soccer tournament and not until 1994 did the country finally qualify for the World Cup finals. Yet Saudi Arabia does have a world championship to its name, courtesy of its Under-17 World Cup winning team in 1989.

Record

World Cup: Never qualified for finals until 1994

Olympic Games: Never gone beyond first round

Under-17 World Cup: Winner 1989

Intercontinental Cup: Finalist 1992

Asian Cup: Winners 1984, 1988; finalist 1992

South Korea

Few Asian countries can rival South Korea in terms of consistent—albeit unspectacular—success over the past 40 years. Not only did the national team win the first two Asian Cups ever held but it has appeared in three subsequent finals. South Korea also has the distinction of having qualified for more World Cups than any of its other Asian brethren. In 1954, it had the misfortune of facing Hungary, which administered a 9-0 pasting, followed by a 7-0 walloping by Turkey. The scores were much closer in 1986, when a very creditable showing by South Korea included a heartbreaking 3-2 loss to Italy. But Korea won few friends, let alone matches, with three drab performances four years later in Italy. Little success has been achieved in the Olympic soccer tournament, even when Seoul hosted the Games in 1988, although before its partition, Korea did reach the quarter-finals in 1948.

Record

World Cup: Never gone beyond first round

Olympic Games: Never gone beyond first round

Under-20 World Cup: Fourth place 1983

Asian Cup: Winners 1956, 1960; finalists 1972, 1980, 1988; third place 1964

Oceania

Apart from Australia and New Zealand, where soccer has been played for more than a century, there are no other significant soccer-playing countries in what remains a FIFA backwater. The **Oceania Football Confederation (OFC)** finally came into being in 1966, but made such little impact that seven years later Australia decided to pull out and attempt to join the Asian Football Confederation instead. Only a subsequent rejection from the AFC, which forced Australia to rejoin the fold, ensured the OFC's survival. An international competition for member countries was arranged in the 1970s, but after two tournaments, the **Oceania Cup** went into hibernation and shows no sign of awaking. A club competition for Oceania teams has never even been attempted. Until FIFA is prepared to grant Oceania at least one automatic berth in the World Cup finals, soccer will never make much of a splash.

Australia

Despite tough competition from cricket, rugby, and Australian rules football, soccer has still made great strides in Australia in recent years. Although a national association was first formed in 1882, the sport made little headway until the 1960s, when a new governing body came into existence and Australia began striving to qualify for the World Cup finals. Success was finally achieved in 1974, when the national team managed to hold West and East Germany to relatively modest 3-0 and 2-0 wins and even gained a goalless tie against Chile. Unfortunately, Australia hasn't been able to repeat the feat since. In the 1994 qualification attempt, the Australians won their initial Oceania group, then beat New Zealand in the Oceania playoff. They then beat Canada in a special playoff and narrowly lost to Argentina in yet another playoff. This team, which featured several outstanding players who are now parading their skills in various European leagues, almost beat Argentina in Sydney, settling for a tie instead, before predictably bowing out in Buenos Aires. Other notable achievements include two consecutive semi-final appearances in the Under-20 World Cup, as well as a highly creditable fourth place finish at the 1992 Barcelona Olympics with its Under-23 team. For many years, domestic Australian soccer was organized on a state-by-state basis, but a national league came into being in 1977.

Record

World Cup: Never gone beyond first round

Olympic Games: Fourth place 1992

Under-20 World Cup: Fourth place 1991, 1993

North American Soccer

When **U.S. Soccer** president **Alan Rothenberg** hired coach **Bora Milutinovich** (the Yugoslavian who coached the Mexican and Costa Rican World Cup teams) to lead the American team in 1991, he promised "to win the next World Cup." Given the country's past championship record, everybody thought he was crazy. But Rothenberg proved to be a man of his word—and it took him only eight months. On 30 November 1991, the United States beat Norway to win the World Cup—the Women's World Cup. North America's only other "world title" had come 87 years earlier, when Canada triumphantly won the gold medal at the 1904 Olympics in St. Louis—though soccer was just an exhibition sport at the time and Canada's only opponents were two American teams.

Soccer is simply not yet a way of life in the United States and Canada as it is in most of Europe and South America. For the last century, North America has been a sleeping giant on the world soccer scene, but at long last it appears that it may be showing some signs of coming to life. The 1994 World Cup was the third in a row in which a North American country participated; the 1996 Olympic soccer tournament will mark the fourth consecutive appearance by the United States; and U.S. and Canadian teams are continually qualifying for FIFA youth tournaments.

Soccer in the United States

Soccer was exported from Britain to America with the first colonists. As early as 1609, the Jamestown settlers were playing a football game similar to the one enjoyed 3,000 miles away on the other side of the Atlantic. Even after America's split from Britain in 1776, the sport developed on a parallel course in both countries. In the mid-19th century, the dispute in Britain between players who wanted to throw the ball with their hands and traditionalists who maintained it should only be kicked with the feet became the source of great controversy in the United States, too. While many Britons defiantly picked up their oval-shaped ball and started to play rugby football, Americans grabbed their pigskin and began playing a game resembling rugby, which they continued to call football. But whereas the ever-increasing popularity of soccer in Britain was largely unaffected by the introduction of rugby, American soccer was gradually submerged by the growing interest in gridiron football, as well as the country's developing love affair with baseball. U.S. soccer has largely been kept alive in the 20th century by immigrants to America who were eager to continue playing their native game. The sport mainly became a bastion of the country's ethnic communities, although even many of them were converted to football, baseball, basketball, and hockey.

The game's organized roots in the United States date back to 1884, the year the **American Football Association (AFA)**, the sport's first U.S. governing body, was formed by a group of British enthusiasts. The following year, the United States played its first international match against neighboring Canada. Factional disputes raged within the AFA until 1914, when the newly formed **United States Football Association (USFA)**—the precursor of today's U.S. Soccer—officially became a member of FIFA.

Although a soccer backwater, the United States still managed to enter teams for both the Olympics and the World Cup. In 1939, a year after many Central American and Caribbean nations had formed their own regional association, the **Confederación Centroamericana y del Caribe de Fútbol (CCCF)**, the United States joined Cuba and Mexico to establish the rival **North American Football Confederation**. Neither body made much impact until both were united in 1961 to create the **Confederación Norte-Centroamericana y del Caribe de Fútbol (CONCACAF)**. Little interest was shown in CONCACAF—other than as a means of attempting to qualify for the World Cup finals—until 1990, when the confederation headquarters were switched from Guatemala City to New York and **Chuck Blazer** of the United States was elected as the confederation's administrative head.

Only in the last three decades has soccer found new visibility in the United States. The catalyst was the creation of the **North American Soccer League (NASL)**, the country's first and only professional outdoor league, in 1968. Even though the NASL collapsed in 1985, the sport has been able to build upon the bedrock of youth soccer participation that the league in part inspired. FIFA hoped to plumb this interest in soccer among America's youth by holding the 1994 World Cup in the United States, although there's universal agreement that only the reestablishment of a professional league can ensure long-term success.

World Cup

Since it was invited to play in FIFA's inaugural World Cup in 1930, the United States has attempted to qualify for every tournament except the one in 1938, when it decided not to compete for fear of suffering the same drubbing it had received four years earlier. At the next World Cup—not held until 1950 because of World War II—the United States not only qualified for the finals but it produced what remains the biggest upset in the history of soccer—a 1-0 win against England. Repeatedly stymied by powerhouse

Mexico, the United States was unable to qualify for the next nine tournaments. It took another 40 years for the United States to return to the finals in 1990, but despite a magnificent performance against Italy, the team lost all three first-round matches.

Olympics

At the 1904 Olympic Games in St. Louis, the United States was represented by two local teams, Christian Brothers College and St. Rose Kickers, who were both beaten by Galt F.C., a club team from Ontario, Canada. Not until 1928 did the United States compete in Olympic soccer again, only to receive an 11-2 lambasting by Argentina, a prophetic indicator of the similarly lopsided score in favor of Argentina when both teams faced each other again two years later in the 1930 World Cup semi-finals.

No soccer tournament was held at the 1932 Olympics in Los Angeles—a telling sign of the sport's lack of importance in this country—but during the next three Olympic Games, the United States lost to Italy every time at the first hurdle, by scores of 1-0, 9-0, and 8-0. Things didn't improve for the battered Americans at Melbourne in 1956, when they fell to Yugoslavia 9-1. Then came the introduction of qualifying tournaments, in which the United States lost to its old nemesis Mexico in 1960, was unable to survive round-robin play against Mexico, Surinam, and Panama in 1964, and got beaten by Bermuda in 1968. Finally, in 1972, the United States managed to qualify, only to finish at the bottom of its first-round group after absorbing defeats by West Germany and Malaysia and tying with Morocco. Four years later, Bermuda embarrassed the U.S. team which once again was disqualified, but the United States turned the tables in 1980 and consequently was set to play in Moscow, until the U.S. government decided to withdraw from the Games to protest the Soviet invasion of Afghanistan.

In 1984, the world came to Los Angeles for the Olympics, giving the United States the chance to stage its first major international soccer tournament. Unfortunately, the national team—now restricted to an Under-23 team in accordance with new FIFA regulations—narrowly missed making it to the quarter-finals after beating Costa Rica, tying with Egypt, and losing to Italy. However, 83,642 fans crammed into Stanford Stadium for one semi-final and 97,451 into Pasadena's Rose Bowl for the other. Then the largest crowd ever to watch a soccer match in the United States—101,799—saw France defeat Brazil in the final at the Rose Bowl. Overall, more than 1.4 million U.S. fans watched the 32 games— an average of almost 45,000 per match.

Four years later, the United States breezed through the qualification tournament, but finished at the bottom of its first-round group in Seoul after losing 4-2 to the Soviet Union, tying with Argentina, and also tying with South Korea. In 1992, the United States reached Barcelona after a record-setting qualifying performance in which the Olympic team outscored its opponents 35-12 and finished three points ahead of Mexico, which it beat both home

and away. After a creditable 2-1 loss to Italy, the U.S. team defeated Kuwait 3-1 and tied Poland 2-2, but this wasn't quite enough to get it through to the next round.

Under-20 World Cup

Although the United States has yet to make much of an impression at either the World Cup or the Olympics, the youth teams have qualified for all but one of FIFA's world championships since the 1990 World Cup—a feat managed by no other country except Italy.

The United States reached the finals of the Under-20 World Cup for the first time in 1981, but failed to get past the first round, losing to Uruguay and Poland and tying with Qatar. Two years later in Mexico, the Americans made it through to the finals again, but fell once more, to Uruguay and Poland, although they achieved a historic first win over Côte d'Ivoire. After failing to qualify in 1985, the Under-20 team won its way to the 1987 championship, but a lone win over Saudi Arabia couldn't offset losses to West Germany and Bulgaria. However, the 1989 team swept past the first round—by defeating East Germany, tying Mali, and losing only to Brazil—and into the quarter-finals, where a 2-1 victory against Iraq set up a semi-final match with much-favored Nigeria, which ended in a 2-1 win for Nigeria. The Americans eventually had to settle for fourth place after another loss to Brazil, but this was still far and away the best performance by any U.S. national team. Qualification eluded the United States in 1991, but the team returned two years later for the finals in Australia, and captured headlines by thrashing Turkey, the top-seeded European team, 6-0, and moving into the quarter-finals—despite a loss to England and a tie with South Korea—in which it had the misfortune to meet Brazil yet again, losing to the eventual winners 3-0.

Under-17 World Cup

Since the Under-17 World Cup tournament was introduced in 1985, the United States has qualified for all five championships for the world's best high school players—an achievement matched only by Australia. Unable to get past the first round in the 1985, 1987, and 1989 competitions, the team opened a few eyes in 1991 by first defeating Italy, the host nation, then Argentina, and finally China. What looked as though it would be a memorable tournament for the United States, however, was derailed by a heartbreaking penalty shootout loss to Qatar after the two teams tied their quarter-final match. Sweet revenge came two years later when a 5-1 rout of Qatar—which was preceded by a tie with the former Czechoslovakia and a loss to Colombia— put the Americans in the quarter-finals once again. But this time Poland ended U.S. hopes with an easy 3-0 win.

Other International Tournaments

Following its newfound interest in and endorsement of CONCACAF in 1990, the United States took immediate action to upgrade the status of the confederation's championship, giving it a glossy new name, the **Gold Cup,** and confounding many experts by waltzing off with the trophy at the inaugural tournament in 1991 by downing a stunned Mexico 2-0 in the semi-final, then defeating Honduras on penalty kicks in the final. Two years later, the United States got its comeuppance when Mexico trounced the American team 4-0 in a frenzied final before 120,000 screaming fans at Azteca Stadium in Mexico City.

Just before this nightmare in Mexico, the United States accompanied its traditional south-of-the-border foe to Ecuador for a historic first appearance in **Copa América**, an international championship previously reserved only for South American nations. Devoid of many of its foreign-based stars (because their European clubs refused to release them to play for the U.S. national team) and wilting under the limelight, the United States couldn't get past the first round. The United States lost to both Ecuador and Uruguay, then inexplicably allowed Venezuela, traditionally the runt of the South American litter, to come back from a 3-0 deficit and force a tie.

In 1992, a new tournament was created, albeit somewhat artificially, by matching up the United States with some of the world's top soccer nations. The Americans won the first **U.S. Cup** in impressive fashion by beating both Ireland and Portugal, then held Italy to a draw, but the following year the competition got a lot tougher. In what American officials stressed would be a dress rehearsal for the 1994 World Cup the following summer, Brazil, Germany, and England joined the United States in a memorable tournament. Brazil had no trouble defeating the American team, but the U.S. players revived memories of their country's famous 1950 victory by dramatically and decisively beating England 2-0. They also caused the Germans to blush a couple of times before star player **Lothar Matthäus** and his team escaped with a 4-3 victory.

Women's World Cup

The United States' most spectacular success was reserved for FIFA's inaugural Women's World Cup, held in China in 1991. The team gave a preview of the fireworks to come by blasting an astonishing 49 goals past five startled opponents in the CONCACAF qualifying competition. After a relatively close encounter with Sweden, which the Americans won 3-2, the U.S. steamroller got into gear, crushing Brazil 5-0 and Japan 3-0, before moving inexorably into the quarter-finals, where the team demolished Chinese Taipei 7-0, with star striker **Michelle Akers-Stahl** scoring a record five goals. Next came a 5-0 semi-final trouncing of Germany—featuring a **Carin Jennings** hat trick—which set up a 2-1 triumph in the final against Norway, with Akers-Stahl's two goals proving critical. America's lethal forward line of Akers-Stahl, Jennings, and team captain **April Heinrichs**, responsible for 20 of the team's 25 goals, was quickly dubbed the "triple-edge sword."

▪▪▪▪▪▪▪▪▪▪▪▪▪▪▪▪▪▪▪▪▪▪▪▪▪▪

Flamboyant former New York Cosmos goalie Shep Messing once posed nude for *VIVA* magazine.

Professional Leagues

Organizing and running a national soccer league in a country as large and diverse as the United States is no easy proposition. Not surprisingly, the history of U.S. soccer is littered with the carcasses of failed leagues. The first such attempt was the **American Soccer League (ASL)**, introduced in 1921 on a supposedly fully professional basis, but in reality the league was restricted to America's East Coast, was semi-professional at best, and barely got noticed among the welter of other American sports. The fortunes of the ASL—forever touted by its supporters as the country's oldest league—have spluttered over the years. The league collapsed in the late 1920s, revived in 1933, folded once more in 1984, and was finally reincarnated again in 1988 for a couple of years before merging with the **Western Soccer League (WSL)** to create the **American Professional Soccer League** (see page **64**).

By far the most successful—and splashiest—effort to create a coast-to-coast professional championship in the United States was the **North American Soccer League (NASL)**. Stimulated by American television coverage of the 1966 World Cup, several business groups decided the time was right for a U.S. league. Unfortunately, the notoriously weak **United States Soccer Football Association (USSFA)** and the **Canadian Soccer Football Association (CSFA)** were unable to channel this creative energy into one entity and eventually two rival leagues set up shop: the **United Soccer Association (USA)**—based on an earlier model provided by the **International Soccer League (ISL)**, which had imported entire foreign teams for a while in the early 1960s—and the **National Professional Soccer League (NPSL)**, composed of teams packed with aging foreign stars. The 1967 season turned out to be a costly standoff in the battle of the acronyms—the USSFA's and CSFA's official backing of the USA league was canceled out by CBS's television coverage of the NPSL. Amid the threat of lawsuits, both leagues finally came to their senses the following year and merged, to form the NASL.

The story of the NASL is one of tumultuous peaks and plunging valleys—from a paltry five teams in 1969 to a thriving 24 between 1978 and 1980, then back down to nine by 1984, the league's swansong season. The NASL hit its high point during the

▪▪▪▪▪▪▪▪▪▪▪▪▪▪▪▪▪▪▪▪▪▪▪▪▪▪

The 1990 World Cup defender Steve Trittschuh became the first American to play in the European Cup on 19 September 1990 when he appeared for Sparta Prague of Czechoslovakia against Moscow Spartak of Russia. The following year, former Fresno State player Geoff Gray cracked the same barrier in the European Cup Winners Cup by playing for Danish club OB Odense against Galway United of Ireland.

In 1990, Dale Mulholland became the first American to play in what was then the Soviet Union's first division.

mid-1970s, with the signing of **Pelé** and **Franz Beckenbauer** by the flamboyant New York Cosmos franchise. Ironically, it was the big-name foreign stars that ultimately spelled the demise of the NASL—first because owners of all the other teams felt under increasing pressure to sign similar caliber players, often losing enormous sums of money in the process (especially when none of the major networks was prepared to offer a lucrative long-term deal to televise NASL matches), but more critically because the league never paid much more than lip service to the importance of developing high-quality American players whom the local fans could identify with and come to idolize. Unfortunately, the NASL was too much about glitz and glamour and not enough about mom and apple pie.

For many people, the NASL's cardinal sin was its incessant tinkering with soccer's hallowed rules. Although the intent was to experiment with ways of making the game more marketable to the American public, the new laws won the NASL few friends elsewhere in the world and eventually undermined the league's credibility. Among the most controversial changes were switching the demarcation for offside from the halfway line to an arbitrary line 35 yards from the goal line; awarding six points for a win, plus a bonus of one point for each goal scored up to a maximum of three; and introducing a "shootout" at the end of every tied match to guarantee fans would see a winner and a loser (the format was essentially the same as today's penalty kick shootout, except that each "shooter" started with the ball on the 35-yard line, then had five seconds to go one-on-one with the goalkeeper and score.

Sadly, the collapse of the NASL scuttled some outstanding teams, who had built a loyal following and promoted soccer in the United States and Canada. Even the heavily bankrolled Cosmos deserve some credit, as do the Tampa Bay Rowdies, the Seattle Sounders, the Vancouver Whitecaps, the Minnesota Kicks, and several others. Some of these franchises tried to continue on in other leagues, but when the NASL's bubble burst, much of the aura surrounding these teams disappeared.

Since the demise of the NASL, a number of regional leagues have attempted to fill the resulting void, most notably including the **Western Soccer Alliance**—soon renamed the Western Soccer League (WSL)—and the ever-resilient American Soccer League (ASL). In 1990, the WSL and ASL merged to form the American Professional Soccer League (APSL), but what began as four divisions of 22 teams shrank to one division of seven teams by 1993, and its future remains extremely uncertain. Plagued by small crowds, unstable franchises, and poor media exposure, the APSL is professional in name only. **Dan Van Voorhis,** owner of the San Francisco Bay Blackhawks, arguably the APSL's most successful franchise, claims to have lost $5 million in the league's first four years of operation, including $2.5 million alone during the 1992 season. The APSL was responsible for introducing another

NASL Championships (known as the Soccer Bowl after 1975)

1967	**USA:** Los Angeles Wolves 6	Washington Whips 5
	NPSL: Baltimore Bays 1	Oakland Clippers 0
	Oakland Clippers 4	Baltimore Bays 1 (Oakland won 4-2 on aggregate)
1968	San Diego Toros 0	Atlanta Chiefs 0
	Atlanta Chiefs 3	San Diego Toros 0 (Atlanta won 3-0 on aggregate)
1969	Kansas City Spurs (championship played on round-robin basis)	
1970	Rochester Lancers 3	Washington Darts 0
	Washington Darts 3	Rochester Lancers 1 (Rochester won 4-3 on aggregate)
1971	Atlanta Chiefs 2	Dallas Tornado 1
	Dallas Tornado 4	Atlanta Chiefs 1
	Atlanta Chiefs 0	Dallas Tornado 2 (Dallas won best-of-3 series 2-1)
1972	New York Cosmos 2	St. Louis Stars 1
1973	Philadelphia Atoms 2	Dallas Tornado 0
1974	Los Angeles Aztecs 4	Miami Toros 3
1975	Tampa Bay Rowdies 2	Portland Timbers 0
1976	Toronto Metros-Croatia 3	Minnesota Kicks 0
1977	New York Cosmos 2	Seattle Sounders 1
1978	New York Cosmos 3	Tampa Bay Rowdies 1
1979	Vancouver Whitecaps 2	Tampa Bay Rowdies 1
1980	New York Cosmos 3	Fort Lauderdale Strikers 0
1981	Chicago Sting 1	New York Cosmos 0
1982	New York Cosmos 1	Seattle Sounders 0
1983	Tulsa Roughnecks 2	Toronto Blizzard 0
1984	Chicago Sting 2	Toronto Blizzard 1
	Toronto Blizzard 2	Chicago Sting 3 (Chicago won best-of-3 series 2-0)

APSL Championships

1990	Maryland Bays 1	San Francisco Bay Blackhawks 1 (Bays won 4-3 on penalties)
1991	Albany Capitals 3	San Francisco Bay Blackhawks 1
	San Francisco Bay Blackhawks 2	Albany Capitals 0
	San Francisco Bay Blackhawks 0	Albany Capitals 0 (mini-game; Blackhawks won 4-3 on penalties)
1992	Colorado Foxes 1	Tampa Bay Rowdies 0
1993	Colorado Foxes 3	Los Angeles Salsa 1

quirky innovation. In 1991, its championship became a best-of-two series, but instead of using the total aggregate score to determine the winner if each team won one match—as the rest of the world does—the new rules called for a 30-minute "mini-game" immediately after the second match, followed by a penalty kick shootout if necessary. This format was abandoned in 1992.

As part of its decision to hold the 1994 World Cup in the United States, FIFA insisted that a full-fledged professional league be in place in North America by 1993. Although he couldn't meet this deadline, **Alan Rothenberg,** president of **U.S. Soccer** and chairman/chief executive officer of **World Cup USA 1994,** is now preparing to wear yet another hat by heading up **Major League Soccer,** a 12-team league tentatively scheduled to play its first season from April to September in 1995. The league hopes to take advantage of the goodwill and positive publicity generated by the 1994 World Cup in the U.S., but many details still need to be worked out before it can become reality. The plan is for the league to become the first division of what will eventually be a three-division setup, with the second and third divisions functioning very much like baseball's minor league system.

In 1977, the Pelé-led New York Cosmos attracted a record North American Soccer League crowd of 77,691 to Giants Stadium for a playoff match against the Fort Lauderdale Strikers. The Cosmos put eight goals past Gordon Banks, the former England goalie widely recognized as one of the greatest ever to play the position.

It's quite a job to convert a baseball stadium into a soccer stadium. According to the *Rocky Mountain News,* when Denver's Mile High Stadium staged an international soccer match between the United States and Uruguay in 1991, it took 30 workers 22 hours over the course of two days to get things into shape. More than 80 tons of sand and 15,000 square feet of grass sod were required, and one section of stands, 13 stories tall and nine million pounds in weight, had to be moved to transform the baseball diamond into a rectangular soccer field.

In 1992, Liz Belyea became the first woman to coach an NCAA men's team when she took over the reins at Cosumnes River College in Sacramento, California. She later went on to coach the University of California at Santa Cruz's men's team.

The **United States Inter-regional Soccer League (USISL),** which began play as a five-team regional indoor league in 1986 but grew to a 39-team nationwide indoor and outdoor league by 1993, has officially received third-division status by U.S. Soccer. It's hoped the APSL will revert to a second division league.

Indoor Soccer

Although soccer has been played indoors all over the world for years, it was considered little more than a recreational pastime until America got hold of the sport and created its very own professional version. The NASL flirted with indoor soccer for virtually its entire tenure, but not until the arrival in 1978 of the **Major Indoor Soccer League (MISL)**—later confusingly shortened to **Major Soccer League (MSL)**—did the sport enjoy its own separate status. Despite its high visibility in such cities as Baltimore and San Diego, the MSL suffered from many of the same maladies that afflicted the NASL—unstable franchises, lack of television coverage, and inept management—and finally gave up the ghost in 1992.

However, it appears that indoor soccer is here to stay. With the passing of the MSL, the indoor mantle was transferred to the nine-year-old **National Professional Soccer League (NPSL),** which began the 1993-94 season with 12 teams in Northeastern and Midwestern cities, and the **Continental Indoor Soccer League (CISL),** which made its debut during the summer of 1993 with six teams located in West Coast and Southwestern cities plus the additional novelty of one from the Mexican city of Monterrey. Both of these operations have deliberately remained small scale in terms of organization and promotion in a conscious effort to avoid the financial instability that bedeviled the MSL.

Played on a field the size of a hockey rink, with boards enclosing the field, allowing the players to rebound the ball at will, indoor soccer in America bears little resemblance to its outdoor cousin—apart from sharing some of the same skills. Nevertheless, FIFA decided to enter the fray in 1989 and hold a **Five-a-Side World Indoor Championship,** at which the United States won a bronze medal. Three years later, the Americans went one better, winning a silver medal after losing in the final to Brazil. This tournament features fields 44 yards long and 22 yards wide with goals six feet high and nine feet wide. A number 4-sized ball is used, but there are no boards, so when it goes out of bounds, FIFA regulations call for the ball to be put back into play with a "kick-in."

College Soccer

Soccer is increasingly making its presence felt in American colleges and universities among both men and women. In 1993, according to the **National Collegiate Athletic Association (NCAA)** and the

NCAA Division 1 Men's Champions

1959	St. Louis University
1960	St. Louis University
1961	West Chester University
1962	St. Louis University
1963	St. Louis University
1964	Navy
1965	St. Louis University
1966	University of San Francisco
1967	Michigan State/St. Louis University
1968	Michigan State/University of Maryland
1969	St. Louis University
1970	St. Louis University
1971	title rescinded
1972	St. Louis University
1973	St. Louis University
1974	Howard University
1975	University of San Francisco
1976	University of San Francisco
1977	Hartwick University
1978	title rescinded
1979	Southern Illinois University-Edwardsville
1980	University of San Francisco
1981	University of Connecticut
1982	Indiana University
1983	Indiana University
1984	Clemson University
1985	UCLA
1986	Duke University
1987	Clemson University
1988	Indiana University
1989	University of Santa Clara/Univ. of Virginia
1990	UCLA
1991	University of Virginia
1992	University of Virginia
1993	University of Virginia

NCAA Division 1 Women's Champions

1982	University of North Carolina
1983	University of North Carolina
1984	University of North Carolina
1985	George Mason University
1986	University of North Carolina
1987	University of North Carolina
1989	University of North Carolina
1990	University of North Carolina
1991	University of North Carolina
1992	University of North Carolina
1993	University of North Carolina

National Association of Intercollegiate Athletics (NAIA), 591 schools fielded a men's soccer team compared to only 553 with a men's football team. Women's soccer teams exist at 385 schools.

Over the years, controversy has swirled around the reluctance of American colleges to play under either FIFA or U.S. Soccer rules, especially on the tenuous issue of substitution (with players allowed to enter and re-enter almost at will). But the standard of play has steadily improved, and many college players have progressed to the professional ranks either with the U.S. national team or in a foreign league. The unprecedented achievement of the University of Virginia in winning the NCAA Division 1 Men's Championship three years in a row from 1991 to 1993 and the astounding year-after-year dominance of the University of North Carolina in the Division 1 Women's Championship have done much to promote soccer at the college level.

Amateur and Youth Soccer

The appeal of soccer among America's immigrant communities at the turn of the century continues to be echoed today at the amateur level. The **U.S. National Open Challenge Cup,** first held in 1914, is still dominated by teams with strong ethnic backgrounds. The same holds true for the **U.S. National Men's Amateur Cup,** which began in 1924. Other notable amateur tournaments include the **U.S. National Women's Amateur Cup** and the **U.S. National Over-30 Cups** for both men and women.

The fastest growing segment of American soccer remains at the youth level. Boys' and girls' teams can compete for national championships in three different age groups: the **McGuire Cup** (boys) and the **Athena Cup** (girls) for under-19s; the **Greer Cup** (boys) and the **National Cup** (girls) for under-17s; and the **Niotis Cup** (boys) and the **Masotto Cup** (girls) for under-16s. In addition, the **Olympic Development Program (ODP)** throughout the United States allows youngsters to try out for district teams in the hopes of working their way up to state teams and then from there moving on to one of four regional teams. Parents of budding soccer stars can expect to pay anywhere between $500 and $2,500 per year for travel and miscellaneous fees depending upon how far their child progresses.

Top U.S. Players

Des Armstrong This talented and versatile defender, noted for his special ability to shut down a dangerous opponent, has been a commanding presence for the United States. Born in Washington, D.C., he later moved to Columbia, Maryland, and became a star in the suburban youth league and at Howard High School before playing four successful seasons at the University of Maryland and helping Virginia's Fairfax Spartans win the 1987 U.S. National Amateur Cup. A member of the U.S. Under-23 team that competed at the 1988 Olympic Games, he recovered from a broken leg while playing in the MISL for the Baltimore Blast and appeared in all three 1990 World Cup games, including a masterful performance guarding **Salvatore Schillaci** and **Gianluca Vialli** in a tough 1-0 loss to Italy. In 1993, he filled in as sweeper in the absence of Marcelo Balboa (see below).

Marcelo Balboa The undisputed leader of the American defense, this tough-tackling sweeper is a tower of strength who was lost to the U.S. team for most of 1993 because of a serious knee injury. A product of the American Youth Soccer Organization program in Southern California, he played two years for San Diego State University, captained America in the 1987 Under-20 World Cup, and then appeared in all three U.S. matches at the 1990 World Cup in Italy. His four seasons in the APSL have been spent with the San Diego Nomads, the San Francisco Bay Blackhawks, and the Colorado Foxes, for whom he won a championship medal in 1992. Second on the all-time U.S. appearances list, he led the national team in total minutes played in both 1991 and 1992.

Paul Caligiuri Forever famous as the player who put the United States into the 1990 World Cup finals with his 40-yard rocket against Trinidad & Tobago in the crucial final qualifier, this hard-working midfielder played all three matches in Italy, scoring America's first World Cup goal in 40 years against Czechoslovakia. Captain of the UCLA team that won the 1985 NCAA title, he played in the 1987 FIFA All-Star Game, performed brilliantly for the United States at the 1988 Olympics, and then became one of the first Americans to play abroad by joining SV Hamburger of the German Bundesliga. In 1990, he helped Hansa Rostock win East Germany's last Oberliga championship before unification, then played briefly for SC Freiburg of the German second division before returning to the United States.

Rick Davis One of the few homegrown stars produced by the NASL, this precocious midfielder made his debut with the New York Cosmos in 1978 and, surrounded by great foreign players, his career quickly flourished. Selected as the NASL's North American Player of the Year in 1979, he was an influential part of the Cosmos team that won the 1980 and 1982 Soccer Bowls and represented the United States in the 1982 FIFA All-Star Game. His career playing internationally for the U.S. began in 1977 and spanned 43 appearances, many as captain, before his retirement in 1989. In 1993, he became general manager of the APSL's Los Angeles Salsa.

Thomas Dooley An inspiring defender/midfielder who loves to move forward and score goals, this German Bundesliga standout became a fixture on the U.S. national team after receiving his American citizenship in 1992 (his father was a World War II serviceman who married a German). After five seasons with Homburg, he moved to 1.FC Kaiserslautern in 1988 and was a key player in its 1991 championship-winning team. His nose for goals was shown in the 1993 U.S. Cup when he scored once against England and twice against his former compatriots.

John Harkes Probably even better known in England than he is in America, this classy midfielder has won many friends on both sides of the Atlantic for his inspirational play. An accomplished youth player in Kearny, New Jersey, where he teamed up with Tony Meola (see below) and Tab Ramos (see below), he won Missouri Athletic Club Player of the Year honors in 1987 at the University of Virginia and quickly gained a spot on the U.S. team at the 1988 Summer Olympics, later helping his country qualify for the 1990 World Cup. It was his sterling performances in Italy that led to his being signed by Sheffield Wednesday of England, where he scored the "Goal of the Year" during the 1990-91 season and played on the team that won the 1991 English League Cup. Two years later, he was back at Wembley Stadium, becoming the first American to score a goal on that turf during the 1993 League Cup and also appearing in the F.A. Cup final the same year. At the start of the 1993-94 season, he was transferred to Derby County of the English first division.

Kasey Keller A revelation since joining the English first-division team Millwall in 1992, Keller has quickly established himself as one of the best goalkeepers in England. His superb displays at the University of Portland earned him a place on the U.S. team that finished fourth in the 1989 Under-20 World Cup, during which he won the prestigious Silver Ball, awarded to the second-best player in the tournament. Chosen to back up U.S. goalie Tony Meola during the 1990 World Cup, he has been locked in a battle for the top spot ever since.

Tony Meola One of the most experienced U.S. players despite his tender age, this imposing goalkeeper made a name for himself at the 1990 World Cup finals in Italy while only 21. He first attracted attention at Kearny High School in New Jersey, where he led his team to the state title in 1986. Three years later, after helping the University of Virginia to share honors with the University of Santa Clara in the 1989 NCAA championship, he won both the Hermann Trophy and the Missouri Athletic Club Player of the Year award, and soon established himself on the national team. He played briefly with Brighton and Watford in England, then moved back to America, performing for the APSL's Fort Lauderdale Strikers in 1991 and winning "Most Valuable Player" honors during the 1991 Gold Cup. In addition to excelling in soccer, Meola was also an outstanding baseball player at Virginia and was drafted as a centerfielder by the New York Yankees, but decided to pursue soccer instead.

Tab Ramos This skillful midfielder, who never seems to stop running, is a vital cog in the American team. Another of the players who first came to the fore in the New Jersey high-school system, he played on the same youth team as John Harkes (see above). Ramos made his international debut at the age of 15 at the 1983 Under-20 World Cup, became a star during his collegiate days at North Carolina State University, and later appeared for the United States at the 1988 Olympics and the 1990 World Cup. Figueras of Spain signed him right after the World Cup, but following two highly successful seasons, he was transferred to fellow second-division team Real Betis, where many knowledgeable soccer observers now consider him the best overseas American player of all.

Claudio Reyna America's latest young phenomenon, this exceptionally gifted midfielder, noted for his amazing passing ability, is widely expected to make a big impact on the U.S. national team. He drew national attention while playing for St. Benedict's Prep High School in Newark, New Jersey, which never lost a game when he played. Since joining the University of Virginia in 1991, he has covered himself in a blaze of glory, leading the team to three consecutive NCAA championship victories and winning the Missouri Athletic Club Player of the Year award in 1992. A member of both the U.S. Under-17 and Under-20 teams, he also played every minute of every game for the Under-23 team at the 1992 Olympics. In 1992, he turned down the opportunity to join Spanish powerhouse Barcelona.

Kyle Rote, Jr. Instead of following in the footsteps of his father, a famous football player, this superb natural athlete instead became the first American to gain national acclaim as a soccer star. In high school, he shone in football, baseball, and basketball, but a football injury at Oklahoma State University prompted a transfer to the University of the South in Tennessee, where he played soccer for the first time. In his first full season with the NASL's Dallas Tornado in 1973, he was "Rookie of the Year," scoring 10 goals in 18 matches. After five more years with Dallas, he played one season for the Houston Hurricane before retiring in 1979 with 44 goals to his name in 150 matches. Although he only made six appearances for the U.S. national team, he received a lot of publicity by winning the "Superstars" competition in 1974, 1976, and 1977.

Roy Wegerle Guaranteed to provide the United States with lots of firepower up front, this speedy striker adds an extra attacking dimension to the national team. Although born in South Africa, he spent his college career at the University of South Florida and was the first player selected in the 1984 NASL draft by the Tampa Bay Rowdies, where he enjoyed one productive season before the league folded. After three seasons with the Tacoma Stars of the MISL, in 1986 he sought fame and fortune in England, playing first for Chelsea, then moving into the first division with Luton Town, where he established himself as a proven goalscorer, before being transferred to Queens Park Rangers, Blackburn Rovers, and Coventry City. After receiving his U.S. citizenship through marriage in 1991, he made his debut for the U.S. team the following year, helping his new teammates win the inaugural U.S. Cup.

Eric Wynalda A scoring sensation when he first joined 1.FC Saarbrücken of the Bundesliga in 1992, this exciting striker has also nabbed some important goals for the United States. An award-winning player on his Westlake Village High School team in Southern California, he was also a standout performer at San Diego State University, graduating to the national team in 1990 and playing in two of the three World Cup matches in Italy (although he lost his temper and was ejected for retaliation against Czechoslovakia). After scoring nine goals in his first 10 matches with Saarbrücken, he went through a lean period and the team was relegated to the second division. He fortunately regained his scoring touch the next season.

Soccer in Canada

Although the Inuit have been playing a primitive form of football on ice called *aqsaqtuk* for hundreds of years, the earliest Canadian reference to soccer as we know it today didn't occur until 1859. Nine years later, the **Montreal Football Club** became the first organization of its kind in the country, and the sport just seemed to be hitting its stride in 1873 with the formation of the **Canadian Football Association.** But then came a thunderbolt. Based on its contacts with Britain, Montreal's McGill University formed a rugby team and in 1874 played a match against Harvard University using the familiar oval ball that transformed sporting history on both sides of the border. Harvard popularized this new game among other northeastern colleges, and it quickly developed into what is now known as American football, while to the north a Canadian version of football started to sweep the country, too.

At first, Canadian soccer was able to resist this brash new sport. Not only did Canada make its international debut in 1885, visiting Newark, New Jersey, to play—and defeat—the United States, but a Canadian team also traveled all the way to the British Isles in 1888 and 1891 to play representative games against England, Scotland, Wales, and Ireland. However, by the turn of the century, Canadian football had become dominant. Although the **Dominion of Canada Football Association,** the forerunner of the present **Canadian Soccer Association,** came into being in 1912, soccer struggled to make any headway. For many years, apart from interest among newly arrived immigrants, the sport enjoyed almost no visibility at all. Not until 1957 did Canada play its first international match at home, and the team's 5-1 defeat of the United States was also its first attempt to qualify for the **World Cup.** However, two emphatic wins by Mexico quickly extinguished any Canadian dreams of making it to the finals.

Canada sat out World Cup qualifying in 1962 and 1966, returning to the fray in 1970, but fell at the very first hurdle. It was the same story in 1974, although four years later the team did win a playoff against the United States and made it through to the final round, only to finish behind Mexico and Haiti. In 1982, Canada started to show some signs of real promise by actually winning its first round of matches ahead of both Mexico and the United States, but in the final round, it couldn't keep pace with Honduras and El Salvador, the eventual qualifiers. But in 1986, Canada took full advantage of Mexico's absence (the country automatically qualified as World Cup hosts) by first winning its second-round group, sweeping aside Guatemala and Haiti, then repeating the feat in the final round, at the expense of Honduras and Costa Rica, to qualify for a World Cup for the one and only time in its history. Predictably, the Canadians lost all three matches—

against France, Hungary, and the Soviet Union—and didn't score a single goal, although it should be noted that none of Canada's opponents managed to put more than two goals past a very well-marshaled defense.

But World Cup play in 1990 took a turn for the worse, with Canada losing to Guatemala both home and away, thus bringing its qualification hopes to a premature end. However, Canada came closer four years later, reaching the final round relatively easily and finishing a strong second to Mexico, thereby sending it into a playoff against the Oceania winner, Australia. But when both teams won 2-1 on their home soil, matters were settled by penalty kicks, with the Aussies ultimately triumphing 4-1.

The Canadian Olympic team has endured even more hardship, only managing to qualify for two soccer tournaments since 1968—and one of these occurred automatically when Montreal hosted the 1976 Summer Games, although defeats by the Soviet Union and North Korea led to Canada's swift elimination. The other occasion, at Los Angeles in 1984, was far more memorable, with Canada's victory against Cameroon, its tie with Iraq, and its loss to Yugoslavia sending it into the quarter-finals, where it held mighty Brazil to a 1-1 draw and only went out on penalty kicks.

Canada has appeared in three **Under-20 World Cups,** only managing to win one match (against Portugal in 1979) and never getting any farther than the first round. Its **Under-17 World Cup** record is even more lackluster: nine matches played in three separate tournaments and nine straight losses.

The sole Canadian victory in the **CONCACAF Championship** came against weak opposition in 1985, and success has so far eluded the team in the more prestigious **Gold Cup**. The 1993 tournament turned out to be a disaster, when Canada was held to a 2-2 draw by tiny Martinique and then lashed 8-0 by Mexico, the worst defeat in its history.

Professional league soccer has proved as difficult to establish in Canada as it has in its neighbor to the south. The initial attempt was made in 1961 with the **Eastern Canada Professional Soccer League (ECPSL),** but this only lasted five seasons before its demise. Prospects seemed much brighter for the **North American Soccer League**—five Canadian cities were represented at one time or another in the NASL's 19-year history. However, Canadian clubs turned out to be just as flighty as American teams. Toronto, for instance, had five different NASL franchises, although one of them, the Metros-Croatia, did win the Soccer Bowl in 1976. Otherwise, only the Vancouver Whitecaps managed to solidify their presence, surviving for 11 seasons and chalking up Canada's only other Soccer Bowl success in 1979.

Three years after the collapse of the NASL in 1985, Canada welcomed its first attempt at a truly national league, but in such an expansive and sparsely populated country, prospects for the **Canadian Soccer League (CSL)** were dim. And sure enough, it

folded in 1993, with three of its strongest teams (Vancouver 86ers, Toronto Blizzard, and Montreal Impact) linking up with the American Professional Soccer League.

Top Canadian Players

Bob Lenarduzzi This exceptionally talented defender spent his entire NASL career with the Vancouver Whitecaps, playing all 11 seasons for the club and appearing in a record 314 matches. Known for his versatility, he managed to play every position on the field, even including a 45-minute stint as a fill-in goalkeeper. In 1978, Lenarduzzi was converted into a midfielder and rose to the challenge by scoring 10 goals. The next season, back in his familiar fullback role, he helped lead the Whitecaps to a Soccer Bowl title. An equally faithful servant for his country, he made almost 50 appearances in a Canadian shirt, including all three matches during the 1986 World Cup, when he anchored a defense that only conceded five goals. He also played a prominent part in his team's dramatic run during the 1984 Olympic soccer tournament. Lenarduzzi left his native Vancouver at the age of 15 to learn the game in England, where he played for Reading for several seasons before returning home. After the demise of the NASL, he joined the Vancouver 86ers as player-coach, leading the team to several Canadian Soccer League championships, and was then appointed coach of the national team in the early 1990s.

Bruce Wilson One of the steadiest left backs ever to play in the North American Soccer League, this tenacious defender turned down an opportunity early in his career to join England's Everton in order to remain in his native Vancouver. After four seasons with the NASL's Vancouver Whitecaps, he was traded to the Chicago Sting and spent a brief period at the New York Cosmos before finishing his career with the Toronto Blizzard. He made 51 appearances for his country, including all of Canada's matches during the 1984 Olympic soccer tournament and the 1986 World Cup finals.

On 5 September 1992, Kevin Pendergast achieved a rare feat by kicking an extra point for Notre Dame in a 42-7 football win over Northwestern at Soldier Field in Chicago and then flying to Bloomington, Indiana, to play in a soccer tournament for Notre Dame against UCLA.

Rene Cassese became the first woman to play in a National Collegiate Athletic Association Division 1 men's soccer match when she appeared for Seton Hall against Rutgers in 1984.

U.S. Olympic soccer player Cobi Jones was astonished to find that the mascot at the 1992 Barcelona Games was also called Cobi, after the Spanish acronym for the Barcelona Olympic Organizing Committee. Cobi, the player, was named by his mother after a little kid who appeared in one of her favorite 1960s movies.

The World Cup

The World Cup is the most popular single sporting event in the world, rivaling the Olympic Games in both size and scope. Some might claim the soccer championship is even bigger and more prestigious, since qualifying play begins a full two years before the grand event. And unlike America's World Series, Super Bowl, or NBA Championship, in which only North American teams vie against one another, the World Cup is a month-long showdown among teams from 24 nations. The winner of the final deciding match can truly claim to be the world soccer champion.

Despite Britain's almost total dominance of soccer in its early years, the idea of a quadrennial international soccer championship based on the Olympic Games was actually the brainchild of two Frenchmen, **Jules Rimet**, president of **FIFA (Fédération Internationale de Football Association)**, and **Henri Delaunay**, general-secretary of the **French Football Federation**. Their dream finally became a reality in 1930, when the first World Cup was held. With the exception of 1942 and 1946, when play was disrupted due to World War II, the World Cup has been held every four years since.

1930

Uruguay

On the strength of its two back-to-back victories in the Olympic Games soccer tournaments of 1924 and 1928, Uruguay was given the prestigious job of hosting the first World Cup—much to the chagrin of Argentina, its powerful neighbor to the south, and virtually all the major European teams. The prospect of a two-week trans-Atlantic voyage kept away most European teams except for France, Belgium, Romania, and Yugoslavia. With so few participants, the need for qualifying matches was eliminated. The competition was thrown open to any country who would send a team—which explains why the United States participated.

Memorable Matches

In the opening round, Argentina played a close game against France. France, behind 1-0, was threatening to tie when, with a full five minutes to play, the Brazilian referee for no apparent reason blew the final whistle. The French protested, and the match eventually resumed. But the damage had been done. The Argentinians were able to regroup and comfortably protect their lead during the remaining minutes.

U.S. Spotlight

The burly American team, made up largely of expatriate Britons, surprised many observers by beating both Belgium and Paraguay with 3-0 in the opening round to win its group and automatically qualify for a semi-final spot against the Argentinian juggernaut. In what proved to be a bruising battle, U.S. defender **Raphael Tracy** broke his leg, goalkeeper **Jim Douglas** was hobbled for most of the match, and midfielder **Andy Auld** got kicked in the mouth. Argentina proceeded to overrun the United States, scoring five second-half goals for a 6-1 rout.

High & Low Points

The Romanian squad that traveled to Uruguay was personally chosen by **King Carol**, the country's biggest soccer fan.

Bolivian referee **Ulysses Saucedo** astonished everyone by awarding Argentina an unprecedented five penalties against crestfallen Mexico—and all five were converted into goals in a 6-3 triumph.

During the U.S. semi-final with Argentina, the U.S. trainer ran on the field to help an injured player. He tripped, breaking a bottle of chloroform in his bag in the process. Overcome by the fumes, he passed out and had to be carried off the field. The injured player was left to fend for himself.

Final: Uruguay 4 Argentina 2

The rivalry between Uruguay and Argentina was so bitter that neither nation could even agree which ball to use for the final. After the coin toss, it was decided that Argentina would choose the ball in the first half; Uruguay, the second half. Playing under tense conditions, with thousands of troops ringing the new Centenary Stadium in Montevideo for crowd control, Uruguay came back from a 2-1 deficit to put on a dazzling second half. The team scored three goals and sent its frenetic fans into delirium. After the victory, the Uruguayan government proclaimed a national holiday. The jubilation in Montevideo, however, was marred by ugly scenes in Buenos Aires, where the Uruguayan Consulate was stoned by irate Argentinians.

Star of the Tournament

José Leandro Andrade, the inspiration for Uruguay's Olympic Games gold medal successes of 1924 and 1928, was coaxed out of retirement for the 1930 World Cup. An incredibly skillful right half, Andrade was the "engine" behind his team, setting up many of the goals. He and teammates **Lorenzo Fernandez** and **Alvaro Gestido** formed what came to be known as *la costilla metallica* ("the iron curtain").

At 12,000 feet above sea level, the Bolivian capital of La Paz is the highest major venue for international soccer.

1934

Italy

Politics, simmering below the surface of the first World Cup, boiled over four years later when Italy's Fascist dictator **Benito Mussolini** won the right to stage the tournament and proceeded to put on a stiflingly nationalistic show. Since all the major European teams, except England, wanted to participate, a qualifying competition was held for the first time. But this newfound interest from the Europeans (contrasted to their attitude four years earlier) so irked Uruguay that it decided to boycott the tournament. After beating Palestine in a qualifying game, Egypt became Africa's first ever finalist.

Memorable Matches

Austria came into the World Cup as one of the favorites, but it had the misfortune to meet Italy in the semi-finals. The legendary "Wunderteam," admittedly past its prime, put on a masterful performance before succumbing to a scrambled goal by **Enrico Guaita.** He was one of three Argentinian-born players whose Italian parentage qualified them to play for their new adoptive country—a source of much controversy.

U.S. Spotlight

The United States found itself in a qualifying group with Cuba, Haiti, and Mexico. Not knowing whether an additional World Cup slot would be open, the team had to head for Rome regardless. It wasn't until three days before the tournament started that the playoff between the U.S. and Mexico finally took

64 Years of World Cup Play

Year	Countries in Qualifying Competition	Europe	South America	Africa	CONCACAF	Asia	Oceania	TOTAL
1930	0	4	7	0	2	0	0	13
1934	32	12	2	1	1	0	0	16
1938	36	13	1	0	2	0	0	16
1950	32	6	5	0	2	0	0	13
1954	38	12	2	0	1	1	0	16
1958	53	12	3	0	1	0	0	16
1962	56	10	5	0	1	0	0	16
1966	71	10	4	0	1	1	0	16
1970	70	10	3	1	2	0	0	16
1974	99	9	4	1	1	0	1	16
1978	106	10	3	1	1	1	0	16
1982	108	14	4	2	2	1	1	24
1986	121	14	4	2	2	2	0	24
1990	112	14	4	2	2	2	0	24
1994	141	13	4	3	2	2	0	24

place, and the Americans clinched their position with a 4-2 win. In the World Cup proper, the U.S. ran headlong into Italy and, much to **Mussolini's** glee, took a 7-1 thrashing. The humiliation was so deep that the team didn't play another international match for 13 years.

High & Low Points

In a literal battle of might, the quarter-final match between Italy and Spain almost degenerated into a brawl. It ended in a 1-1 tie, with no fewer than seven Spaniards and four Italians nursing injuries bad enough to keep them out of the following day's replay. But the worst was yet to come. In the second match, Spain's two fullbacks ran into each other, knocking themselves unconscious, and two Spanish goals were disallowed by the Swiss referee (whose incompetence later led to his suspension) before Italy's **Giuseppe Meazza** headed in the winning goal.

Argentina, fearing that its best players would defect to Italian league teams, sent a reserve team to the finals instead. The Argentinians paid dearly for the action: Sweden soundly defeated them in the first round.

Final: Italy 2 Czechoslovakia 1

In what promised to be a duel between great goalies—**Frantisek Plánicka** for Czechoslovakia and **Giampiero Combi** for Italy—Czechoslovakia took a surprise 1-0 lead with 20 minutes to play. Soon after, when a Czech shot hit the post, a shocking upset appeared in the making. But the physically intimidating Italians regrouped and tied the game with eight minutes left. A doubtful shot on goal by **Raimondo Orsi** swerved and dipped past an astonished Plánicka. In the first World Cup final to go into overtime, Italy's **Angelo Schiavio** dribbled past an exhausted Czech defender to score the winning goal.

Star of the Tournament

Italy's Giuseppe Meazza began his prolific career as a center forward (a striker), but during the finals he switched to inside right (more of a midfield role). This explains why he scored only two goals during the tournament, although the latter was a crucial one in the quarter-final against Spain. But it was his guile and artistry that made "Peppino"—as the fans affectionately called him—such a feared player. A master dribbler, he was famous for his surging runs and explosive speed.

1938

France

With war clouds looming over Europe, soccer suffered casualties of its own. Absent from the World Cup in 1938 were teams from Austria, which was now annexed into Germany following the *Anschluss;* Spain, torn apart by civil war; Argentina, upset at not being chosen as host nation; and Uruguay, still piqued over the European snub in

1930. Brazil was the sole South American representative, and the Dutch East Indies became the first Asian country to compete. Cuba automatically qualified when all its Caribbean and Central American rivals withdrew.

Memorable Matches

Brazil's first-round encounter against Poland had all the soccer excitement you could ask for. Brazilian striker **Leônidas** (playing in his bare feet) scored a hat trick in the first half, **Ernest Willimowski** staged a second-half comeback for Poland by notching a hat trick of his own and tying the score 4-4, and Leônidas, the "Black Diamond," and Willimowski scored one more apiece in a pulsating 30 minutes of overtime before Brazil's **Romeu** finally scored the winning goal.

U.S. Spotlight

The United States drew a qualification group that seemed to offer it an automatic berth in the finals. But the Americans, still smarting from the Italian drubbing four years earlier, withdrew without playing a game.

High & Low Points

Brazil followed up its thriller against Poland with a vicious match against Czechoslovakia in which the Czech goalie Frantisek Plánicka broke his arm, teammate **Oldrich Nejedly** broke his leg—after being ejected from the game—and two more players, one from each team, also received their marching orders. The result was a 1-1 draw. Robbed of its two star players, Czechoslovakia bowed in the replay, 2-1. Brazil was so confident it would beat Italy in the semi-final that it kept Leônidas out of the game to save him for the final. Without the tournament's leading scorer, Brazil slumped to a 2-1 defeat.

Final: Italy 4 Hungary 2

Famous for giving a Fascist salute to the crowd before each match, the Italian team proved an even stronger force than four years earlier. This was due largely to its superb manager **Vittorio Pozzo**, the continuing presence of Giuseppe Meazza, and several new star forwards. Hungary managed to equalize an early Italian goal, but Italy quickly romped to a 3-1 half-time lead, and although Hungary scored again in the second half, **Silvio Piola** soon put the game to rest with his second goal.

Star of the Tournament

The sheer strength and aerial supremacy of Silvio Piola perfectly complemented the more subtle skills of Guiseppe Meazza. A classic center forward in every sense, Piola was at peak performance during the tournament, scoring five goals and assisting on several others. It was Piola's surging run against Brazil in the semi-final that provoked a desperate foul by a Brazilian defender and the awarding of a penalty, from which Meazza scored Italy's decisive second goal.

1950

Brazil

After a 12-year hiatus, attributed to World War II and its aftermath, the World Cup returned to South America. A major reason for the return was the massive new Maracanà Stadium in Rio de Janeiro with its awesome capacity of 200,000. Once again European participation was spotty, with many countries unwilling to travel the huge distances between matches in Brazil, but England at long last decided to enter the fray. Uruguay also returned to the fold, while temperamental Argentina withdrew in a huff again.

Memorable Matches

In two breathtaking displays of attacking soccer, Brazil demolished Sweden, 7-1, and then Spain, 6-1. The brilliant **Ademir** scored four goals in the first match and chipped in with a pair in the second. So lopsided were the matches that to avoid running up the score (and further humiliating their opponents), the gifted Brazilians entertained their fans by demonstrating their ball-control skills.

U.S. Spotlight

Despite 6-2 and 6-0 hammerings by Mexico, a win and a tie against Cuba in the qualifying tournament was sufficient to send the Americans to Brazil. Against all odds they held a 1-0 lead against Spain until the last 10 minutes of play, when they collapsed and conceded three goals. The same fate seemed inevitable against England at Belo Horizonte. But in what remains the greatest upset in World Cup history, the United States embarrassed England with a shocking 1-0 win. Indeed, the English played beneath their potential, and as **Sir Stanley Rous,** later to become FIFA president, acknowledged: "The Americans were faster, fitter, better fighters." The crucial goal was headed in by a naturalized Haitian named **Larry Gaetjens,** who was later carried from the field by exultant Brazilians. The United States winning streak came to an end with a 5-2 defeat by Chile in its final match, thus eliminating it from further contention.

High & Low Points

Thanks to last-minute withdrawals, only 13 countries qualified for the finals, which resulted in uneven groups of initial round-robin play. Most countries had to play three highly competitive games in as many different cities, but somehow Uruguay ended up having to play just one game against hapless Bolivia—a predictable 8-0 rout.

The immense but unfinished Maracanà Stadium made its presence felt when talented Yugoslavian **Rajko Mitic** bumped into an exposed steel girder as he was leaving the locker room before the match against mighty Brazil. By the time he got bandaged up and sent onto the field, Brazil had a comfortable 2-0 lead.

Final: Uruguay 2 Brazil 1

Actually, this wasn't a true final at all. Instead of single elimination matches, excessive tinkering by the World Cup organizers produced a final round-robin pool of four countries. Brazil and Uruguay, the two South American superpowers, swept away the competition and awaited their decisive encounter. In front of a mammoth crowd of 199,850 (still a world record), Brazil was the heavy favorite. But a brilliant defensive performance by Uruguay stifled the prolific scoring Brazilian forwards, and two opportunistic goals by **Juan Schiaffino** and **Alcide Ghiggia** in the second half canceled out an earlier Brazilian score. Back in Montevideo, eight heart attack deaths were attributed to the shocking news.

Star of the Tournament

Brazil boasted one of the best forward lines of all time: **Jair, Zizinho,** and Ademir. But it was Ademir who really stole the show in 1950. A supremely talented player, noted for his blazing speed and dribbling, Ademir led all scorers with nine goals. In his 37 international appearances for Brazil, he netted 32 times, an amazing striking rate.

1954

Switzerland

Scenic Switzerland, home of FIFA, was a politically correct choice to host the finals, but its stadiums and facilities proved barely adequate for the job. This was soon forgotten amid the displays of attacking soccer and the sheer number of goals. South Korea qualified for the finals only to become sacrificial lambs in 9-0 and 7-0 thrashings by Hungary and Turkey, respectively. Uruguay and Brazil were South America's lone standard-bearers. This was the first World Cup to be televised in Europe.

Memorable Matches

A searingly hot day in Lausanne produced a barrage of goals in a quarter-final encounter between Austria and Switzerland. The Swiss scored three early goals, and Austria replied with a trio of its own in a blistering three-minute span. But the goals kept flowing—Austria led 5-4 at half-time and eventually triumphed 7-5 (a record World Cup aggregate score).

Four days later, the rain poured down in Lausanne, but nevertheless Uruguay and Hungary put on a truly spectacular show. Hungary took a 2-0 lead thanks to the remarkable duo of **Zoltan Czibor** and **Nandor Hidegkuti,** but Uruguay roared back with two goals and the match went into overtime. Two headers by the amazing **Sandor Kocsis** gave Uruguay its first World Cup defeat.

U.S. Spotlight

The Americans fell to their usual two defeats (3-1 and 4-0) in qualifying play against Mexico. Even 3-0 and 3-2 wins over Haiti, the other member of its group, were not sufficient to qualify them for World Cup finals play. Given the growing number of nations competing for a place in the finals, only one team was allowed to enter from North and Central America.

High & Low Points

The pressure on Brazil and Hungary in their quarter-final match was so intense that the game degenerated into what is infamously called the "Battle of Berne." Things literally started to unravel when a Brazilian defender tore off Hidegkuti's shorts while he was busy scoring Hungary's first goal. After referee **Arthur Ellis** awarded a controversial penalty, which Sandor Kocsis then converted to put Hungary up 3-1, all hell broke loose. Following **Julinho's** goal, which made the score 3-2, **Jószef Bozsik** of Hungary and **Nilton Santos** of Brazil traded blows and were both ejected. Then **Humberto** kicked a Hungarian and he, too, was sidelined. Kocsis' header wrapped up Hungary's 4-2 win a minute later, but after the match the incensed Brazilians rushed into their opponents' locker room to continue the brawl. Incredibly, FIFA refused to take disciplinary action against either team.

Final: W. Germany 3 Hungary 2

In the first round, the wily German manager **Sepp Herberger** played his reserves against Hungary's all-conquering "Magic Magyars" and was unfazed by the resulting 8-3 blowout. **Ferenc Puskás,** Hungary's greatest player, got injured in the game, but he returned for the final, where he was expected to put West Germany firmly in its place again. However, Puskás was a shadow of his former self, and Hungary underestimated the ever-improving Germans. Hungary raced to a 2-0 lead, but Herberger's men battled back and quickly equalized. Goalie **Toni Turek** single-handedly held Kocsis, Hidegkuti, and company at bay before **Helmut Rahn** put West Germany in front with six minutes to go. Puskás then quickly got the ball in the net, but it was controversially ruled offside, and Hungary suffered its only loss in a string of 49 matches stretching from 1950 to 1956.

Star of the Tournament

Arguably the greatest header, Sandor Kocsis was an acrobatic performer who earned the nickname "Golden Head." But he was certainly no slouch with his feet, either. In the first round Kocsis scored a hat trick against South Korea and then four goals against West Germany. He followed with two goals apiece in Hungary's quarter- and semi-final matches to take his final tally to 11. His seven hat tricks in inter-national play are a world record he shares with **Pelé.**

1958

Sweden

The World Cup entered the television era more popular than ever before. A record 53 countries signed up for the 1958 tournament, and the 89 qualification matches alone attracted more than four million fans. But finding an opponent for politically ostracized Israel proved almost impossible, and it took FIFA gerrymandering to arrange a home-and-away series against Wales, previously eliminated but given a reprieve in a special lottery. Wales duly eliminated Israel and qualified along with Britain's other three representatives (England, Scotland, and Northern Ireland)—the only time this has ever happened. Competing for the first time, too, was the USSR, while Argentina returned after a 28-year absence.

Memorable Matches

Much to everyone's surprise, Wales made it through the first round, eliminating Hungary in a play-off, and met Brazil in a quarter-final that turned out to be a titanic struggle. The ferocious Welsh defense held out until late in the match when a 17-year-old phenomenon named Pelé scored a goal that he still considers the most important of his career.

Pelé left no one in any doubt about his future potential with a magnificent second-half hat trick in Brazil's 5-2 semi-final triumph against France. The redoubtable French held their own in the first half, but when center half **Bob Jonquet** left the match injured, the floodgates opened.

U.S. Spotlight

Two more U.S. thrashings (6-0 and 7-2) at the hands of Mexico were followed by an even more embarrassing 5-1 licking and a 3-2 home defeat by Canada. The U.S. team was anchored firmly at the bottom of its qualification group. Things could only get better.

High & Low Points

French center forward **Just Fontaine** went on an incredible scoring tear during the tournament, finishing up with an amazing 13 goals in six matches, including four in the third-place match against West Germany. To this day, his record remains unbroken.

When two of Northern Ireland's three first-round matches were scheduled on a Sunday, its national soccer association asked the team to boycott these matches—a request that was politely rejected.

Final: Brazil 5 Sweden 2

Sweden turned out to be a perfect host during the tournament, delighting its fans with a series of superbly skillful performances. But in the final, the team was completely overmatched by a Brazilian side at the very top of its form. Brazil's revolutionary new 4-2-4 formation steamrolled Sweden just as it had done to France in the semi-final. After **Nils Liedholm's** fourth-minute tally for Sweden, the two **Santoses, Djalma** and **Nilton,** shut down Sweden's forwards for the rest of the match, and the incomparable **Garrincha** took over, laying on two goals for **Vavá** before Pelé stole the show again with two memorable goals.

Star of the Tournament

Pelé's play made the headlines, but the mastermind behind Brazil's dazzling success was **Didi.** A dominating midfielder, this 30-year-old veteran had the tournament of his life. He orchestrated the proceedings, providing an endless stream of defense-splitting passes for Pelé, Garrincha, Vavá, and **Zagalo.** Didi was also famous for his amazing banana kicks, which terrorized defensive walls the world over.

1962

Chile

South America was itching to stage another World Cup, so when Chile appealed for help after being devastated by a terrible series of earthquakes, FIFA offered it the ultimate prize. The country only possessed four stadiums, but Santiago's at least was brand new. The hosts—borrowing a leaf from Sweden's book—raised their game to new heights. However, the prospect of a long trip to distant Chile only attracted three more qualifying countries than in 1958. Except for games involving Brazil and Chile, attendance overall was disappointingly low, perhaps due to the defensive tone of so many matches—a stark contrast to four years earlier.

Memorable Matches

After storming to an early 3-0 lead against Colombia, the USSR looked ready for a rout. The South Americans managed to score just before half-time, but the Soviets soon reestablished their three-goal margin. Then the USSR's legendary goalkeeper, **Lev Yashin,** committed an extraordinary series of blunders, and Colombia scored three times to tie the score at 4-4. With the Colombians now on the rampage, Yashin steeled himself, recovered his touch, and made several world-class saves to dramatically stem the tide. Neither team could break the 4-4 tie.

U.S. Spotlight

After Canada withdrew from its initial qualifying group, the United States came face-to-face with its old rival Mexico. This time the Americans played well, holding the powerful Mexicans at home 3-3, and then losing on the road by the relatively close score—for them—of 3-0.

High & Low Points

Incensed by a derogatory Italian newspaper article and buoyed by a partisan home crowd, Chile threw everything it had against Italy—quite literally, when star winger **Leonel Sánchez** broke **Humberto**

Maschio's nose with a stunning left hook. Everyone in the stadium (plus a huge television audience) saw what happened except, apparently, the referee, who took no action. The irate Italians retaliated, only to have two players ejected. To add insult to injury, Chile then cashed in by scoring two goals.

The Brazilian president was such a big soccer fan that he supposedly listened to radio coverage of his team's semi-final against Chile on headphones while attending mass.

Final: Brazil 3
Czechoslovakia 1

The final proved to be as disappointing as the whole tournament. After an early Czech goal, scored by the dependable **Josef Masopust,** Brazil gradually worked its way back into the match. Both Garrincha and Didi played below par, but **Amarildo,** substituting for Pelé, who suffered a severe muscle pull in the first round, took advantage of a mistake by the Czech goalkeeper **Schroiff** to tie the score. In the second half **Zito** put Brazil ahead, and when Schroiff lost a lob by Djalma Santos in the sun, Vavá took advantage of a simple goal.

Star of the Tournament

Garrincha had played magnificently in 1958, but in this World Cup the explosive right winger really outdid himself. Born Manuel Francisco dos Santos, he was given the nickname "Garrincha" (Portuguese for "little bird") after a childhood battle with polio left one of his legs slightly deformed. He overcame this adversity to become one of the greatest dribblers in the world. In the quarter-final against England, Garrincha started the scoring off with a header, then added another goal with a viciously swerving shot. He gave Chile the same dazzling treatment in the semi-final, bagging another two goals. Only in the final did he fail to leave his imprint on a match.

1966

England

The country where modern soccer originated finally got to host a World Cup and the English tournament was the first to receive truly global television coverage. The final was viewed by more than 400 million people around the world, including the first network audience in the United States. This was also the first World Cup in which the previous champions (Brazil) and the host nation (England) automatically qualified for the finals. Another notable first was Australia's participation in the qualifying tournament (only to get soundly defeated by North Korea). The one major blot was the mass exodus of 16 African nations in protest of FIFA's reluctance to guarantee an African team in the finals.

Memorable Matches

After flabbergasting Italy, North Korea went on to meet Portugal, one of the most exciting teams in the tournament, in the quarter-finals. Once again an

1994 World Cup

First Round

A

⊕ **Colombia vs. Romania**
Los Angeles, June 18

⊕ **USA vs. Switzerland**
Detroit, June 18

⊕ **USA vs. Colombia**
Los Angeles, June 22

⊕ **Romania vs. Switzerland**
Detroit, June 22

⊕ **USA vs. Romania**
Los Angeles, June 26

⊕ **Switzerland vs. Colombia**
San Francisco, June 26

B

⊕ **Cameroon vs. Sweden**
Los Angeles, June 19

⊕ **Brazil vs. Russia**
San Francisco, June 20

⊕ **Brazil vs. Cameroon**
San Francisco, June 24

⊕ **Russia vs. Sweden**
Detroit, June 24

⊕ **Russia vs. Cameroon**
San Francisco, June 28

⊕ **Brazil vs. Sweden**
Detroit, June 28

C

⊕ **Germany vs. Bolivia**
Chicago, June 17

⊕ **Spain vs. South Korea**
Dallas, June 17

⊕ **Germany vs. Spain**
Chicago, June 21

⊕ **South Korea vs. Bolivia**
Boston, June 23

⊕ **Bolivia vs. Spain**
Chicago, June 27

⊕ **Germany vs. South Korea**
Dallas, June 27

D

⊕ **Argentina vs. Greece**
Boston, June 21

⊕ **Nigeria vs. Bulgaria**
Dallas, June 21

⊕ **Argentina vs. Nigeria**
Boston, June 25

⊕ **Bulgaria vs. Greece**
Chicago, June 26

⊕ **Greece vs. Nigeria**
Boston, June 30

⊕ **Argentina vs. Bulgaria**
Dallas, June 30

E

⊕ **Italy vs. Ireland**
New York, June 18

⊕ **Norway vs. Mexico**
Washington, June 19

⊕ **Italy vs. Norway**
New York, June 23

⊕ **Mexico vs. Ireland**
Orlando, June 24

⊕ **Ireland vs. Norway**
New York, June 28

⊕ **Italy vs. Mexico**
Washington, June 28

F

⊕ **Belgium vs. Morocco**
Orlando, June 19

⊕ **Netherlands vs. Saudi Arabia**
Washington, June 20

⊕ **Saudi Arabia vs. Morocco**
New York, June 25

⊕ **Belgium vs. Netherlands**
Orlando, June 25

⊕ **Morocco vs. Netherlands**
Orlando, June 29

⊕ **Belgium vs. Saudi Arabia**
Washington, June 29

First-Round Play

*I*n the first round, teams from 24 countries are divided into six groups of four countries each. *Every* team plays its three group opponents once on a round-robin basis. *To* encourage more aggressive soccer, **FIFA** changed the points structure for the 1994 World Cup. *Winning* teams earn three points (instead of the traditional two); teams that tie receive one point; and no points are given for a loss.

Second Round & Beyond

*S*ixteen countries—the top teams from each group and the four third-place teams that have scored the most points—advance to the second round. The second round, quarter-finals, semi-finals, and the final are decided by single-elimination matches.

Second Round

Quarter-Finals

Semi-Finals

Semi-Finals

Quarter-Finals

Second Round

🕑 *July 2nd*
Washington
GROUP C Runner-up
GROUP A Runner-up

🕑 *July 5th*
Boston
GROUP D Winner
3rd Best Team in B, E, F

🕑 *July 2nd*
Chicago
GROUP C Winner
3rd Best Team in A, B, F

🕑 *July 5th*
New York
GROUP E Winner
GROUP D Runner-up

🕑 *July 9th*
Boston
BOSTON Winner
WASHINGTON Winner

🕑 *July 10th*
New York
NEW YORK Winner
CHICAGO Winner

🕑 *July 13th*
New York
BOSTON Winner
NEW YORK Winner

🕑 *July 17th*
World Cup Final
Los Angeles
LOS ANGELES Winner
NEW YORK Winner

🕑 *July 16th*
Third Place
Los Angeles
LOS ANGELES Loser
NEW YORK Loser

🕑 *July 13th*
Los Angeles
SAN FRANCISCO Winner
DALLAS Winner

🕑 *July 10th*
San Francisco
LOS ANGELES Winner
DALLAS Winner

🕑 *July 9th*
Dallas
ORLANDO Winner
SAN FRANCISCO Winner

🕑 *July 3rd*
Los Angeles
GROUP A Winner
3rd Best Team in C, D, E

🕑 *July 3rd*
Dallas
GROUP F Runner-up
GROUP B Runner-up

🕑 *July 4th*
Orlando
GROUP F Winner
GROUP E Runner-up

🕑 *July 4th*
San Francisco
GROUP B Winner
3rd Best Team in A, C, D

enormous upset seemed to be in the making when the North Koreans swept to a 3-0 lead in the first 20 minutes—until the unstoppable **Eusébio** rallied Portugal for five straight goals, four of which he scored personally.

In the semi-finals, Portugal faced England, just getting into high gear after three spluttering first-round matches. The spotlight was on Eusébio once more, but England's **Nobby Stiles** kept such a tight rein on him that his only significant contribution was a penalty score toward the end. A superbly well-organized English side triumphed with goals from skipper **Bobby Charlton** and the emerging new talent, **Geoff Hurst.**

U.S. Spotlight

In its best performance in many years, the Americans beat Honduras 1-0 at home, held the same team to a 1-1 draw in Tegucigalpa, and tied Mexico 2-2 in the United States. But losing 2-0 to its old nemesis in Mexico City meant that the United States again couldn't get past the first round of the **Confederación Norte-Centroamericana y del Fútbol (CONCACAF)** qualifying competition.

High & Low Points

Italy got the shock of its life in the first round when, needing just a tie to advance to the quarter-finals, it conceded a goal before half-time to North Korea's **Pak Doo Ik** and then ran up against an iron-tight North Korean defense in the second half. An embarrassed Italian team flew back to Rome, where indignant fans pelted them with rotten fruit and profanities.

In a violent quarter-final encounter between Argentina and England, the Argentinian captain **Antonio Rattin** was ejected for persistently arguing with the referee's decisions. The dissent continued, however, and it was a full 10 minutes before Rattin could eventually be persuaded to leave the field. After the match, England's Manager **Alf Ramsey** described the Argentinians as "animals"—a remark that is controversial to this day.

Final: England 4 W. Germany 2

The tension in Wembley Stadium was thick as England set about fulfilling its dream of winning the Cup in front of its fans. An early goal by **Helmut Haller** was quickly canceled out by Geoff Hurst's header, and England seemed to have won the game when **Martin Peters** scored shortly after half-time. But in the final minute the Germans somehow bundled the ball into the net for a dramatic equalizer. In overtime, Hurst scored what remains the most controversial goal in a World Cup final and then put the game beyond the Germans with a last-minute strike to notch his hat-trick—a feat no other player has since managed to accomplish in a World Cup final.

Star of the Tournament

Until he ran up against England's Nobby Stiles in the semi-finals, Portugal's Eusébio reigned supreme throughout the tournament. The Mozambiquan-born striker, dubbed "the new Pelé," used his lightning speed and ball skills to score a tournament-leading nine goals, including four that turned the tide against the upstart North Koreans. The top scorer in the Portuguese League for nine consecutive seasons (1964-73), Eusébio later played in the United States for the **American Soccer League's Rhode Island Oceaneers** and the **North American Soccer League's Boston Minutemen** in 1975, the championship-winning **Toronto Metros-Croatia** in 1976, and the **Las Vegas Quicksilvers** in 1977.

1970

Mexico

The stifling heat, oppressive humidity, and thin air of Mexico proved even more of a handicap when many of the matches were held in the afternoon to accommodate European television viewers. A new rule allowed teams to make two player substitutions instead of one. Unfortunately, political problems surfaced again: after winning its Asia/Oceania group, Australia was persuaded to play a home-and-away series against Rhodesia in Mozambique. Then, with another win under its belt, Australia had to meet another politically sensitive opponent, Israel, which ultimately stopped it in its tracks. At last Africa was guaranteed one qualifier, and Morocco became the continent's first representative in the finals since 1934. El Salvador's joy at landing in the finals was clouded by the infamous "Fútbol War" with neighboring Honduras.

Memorable Matches

The quarter-final match-up between England and West Germany was an exciting repeat of the 1966 final. The English seemed to have the game under control after taking a comfortable 2-0 lead, but then goalkeeper **Peter Bonetti**—replacing the incomparable **Gordon Banks,** out with food poisoning—let in a soft **Franz Beckenbauer** shot. **Uwe Seeler** equalized, sending the match into overtime. Then, **Gerd Müller** exacted sweet revenge for events four years earlier with the game-winning goal.

West Germany's semi-final match against Italy was equally thrilling. A goal behind with just one minute remaining, West Germany headed into overtime thanks to **Karl-Heinz Schnellinger's** last-gasp goal. Although both teams were completely drained, they continued attacking with vengeance. Müller scored twice for West Germany, while Italy uncharacteristically powered in three goals. The decisive factor in Italy's win may have been the dislocated collar bone Beckenbauer received after a heavy tackle; he refused to leave the field, and continued playing with his arm in a sling.

U.S. Spotlight

Since Mexico automatically qualified for the World Cup as the host team, the greatest obstacle to U.S. chances was removed. The team won the first round of its initial qualifying group with two wins against

Bermuda and then gained a two-game split with Canada, however, only to lose twice to Haiti in the second round.

High & Low Points

Dour England, under manager Sir Alf Ramsey, was not warmly received in Mexico. It didn't help matters any that en route to the World Cup, skipper **Bobby Moore** was arrested in Colombia for purportedly stealing a bracelet from a jewelry store. It turned out he had been framed—a U.S. senator even suggested possible CIA involvement. Although vindicated, the damage had been done. Mexican fans showed their displeasure with the Brits by mounting a noisy vigil outside England's hotel the night before the team's first-round match with Brazil.

The English team kept a stiff upper lip, but lost to Mexico, despite a save by **Gordon Banks** which many believe is still the greatest in World Cup history. Banks launched himself and contorted to tip Pelé's header over the bar.

Final: Brazil 4 Italy 1

Brazil's superiority was clear when Pelé rose acrobatically to head in the first goal, and although **Roberto Boninsegna** did score the tying goal, courtesy of an inappropriate **Clodoaldo** back-heel, the Italians were completely overwhelmed in the second half. The midfield trio of Pelé, **Gerson,** and Clodoaldo feeding the forward line of **Jairzinho, Tostão,** and **Roberto Rivelino** was unstoppable, and Brazil cantered home with goals by Gerson, Jairzinho, and center-back **Carlos Alberto.**

Star of the Tournament

After being shut down in the 1966 tournament by the Bulgarians and the Portuguese, Pelé had vowed never to play in another World Cup. But fortunately he relented four years later and lit up the competition with a positively magical series of performances. In the first round, standing just in front of the half-way line, he audaciously lobbed the Romanian goalkeeper and came within a whisker of scoring. Then on a ball crossed into the penalty area against Uruguay, he faked out a bewildered goalie, ran around him, and rammed the ball toward the goal—only to see it miss by inches. After retiring in 1974, Pelé signed a lucrative contract with the **New York Cosmos** the following year and delighted U.S. fans for another two-and-a-half years.

The 12 nations who competed in the first Women's World Cup in 1991 managed to score a total of 99 goals in 26 games—an average of 3.8 goals per game. The previous year their male counterparts had racked up just 115 goals in 52 games for an average of 2.2 per game.

The Dail, the Irish parliament, voted to adjourn proceedings on the afternoon of Ireland's 1994 World Cup qualifying match against Lithuania so that members could watch their nation's team in action.

1974

West Germany

With the shocking terrorist incident at the 1972 Munich Olympics still fresh in everybody's mind, the West Germans introduced unparalleled security precautions. Many big names didn't even make it to the finals. England was humbled in the qualifying tournament by Poland, and the USSR, after being held to a goalless draw at home by Chile, refused to travel to Santiago for the return match—they balked, supposedly, because the stadium had been used to house political prisoners. Zaire became Africa's first sub-Saharan qualifier, but not before Morocco refused to play against the team in protest of the refereeing in its first encounter. An earlier match between Nigeria and Ghana had to be called off due to crowd disturbances. Haiti's presence in the finals was tainted by the fact that in a crucial qualifying game with Trinidad, a Salvadoran referee disallowed four Trinidad goals. The official was summarily suspended, but the result stood.

Memorable Matches

Fresh from its triumph four years earlier, Brazil needed a win against Holland for a place in the final. This time around, Brazil relied on brawn and defense. By contrast, the free-flowing Dutch—known for their "total soccer" approach in which every player needed to be able to attack and defend—required just a draw. On a rainy night in Dortmund, **Paulo Cesar** and **Jairzinho** missed easy first-half chances, and when Brazil then resorted to familiar roughhouse tactics, center back **Luis Pereira** was ejected, and Holland roared into life with goals from the two **Johans, Neeskens** and **Cruyff.**

It was the same story with West Germany and Poland: the former only needed a tie, the latter had to win. It rained even harder in Frankfurt, but despite huge puddles all over the field, both teams put on an impressive show. West Germany's stocky goal-poacher **Gerd Müller** got the vital strike and **Sepp Maier** put on a virtuoso goalkeeping display to shut down the Poles.

U.S. Spotlight

With Mexico returning to qualifying play, the United States lapsed back into its old ways, losing twice to its rival south of the border and once to Canada. It finished at the bottom of its group.

High & Low Points

Zaire failed to score a single goal and conceded 14 goals in three games, including a record 9-0 defeat against Yugoslavia. This match was notable for the ejection of a Zaire player who rushed out of a defensive wall during a Yugoslavian free kick to kick the ball into the stands.

Haiti's center back **Ernst Jean-Joseph** earned the ignominious distinction of being the first player to fail a World Cup drug test. Sent home in disgrace, he was beaten up by enraged Haitian army officers who imprisoned him in a local German hotel.

Italy, still stuck in its defensive shell, played poorly in the early going. Needing a win against Poland to advance to the next round, the team was alleged to have offered bribes to some Polish players. However, Italy ended up losing 2-1, and all allegations were later recanted.

Final: W. Germany 2 Holland 1

What promised to be a memorable match between two disciples of total soccer got off to a sensational start at the kick-off when Johan Cruyff dribbled his way into the German penalty box, only to be brought down by **Uli Hoeness**. Johan Neeskens promptly converted the first-ever penalty kick in a World Cup final. The Dutch returned the compliment later in the half, when **Bernd Hölzenbein** was brought down, allowing teammate **Paul Breitner** to score a penalty shot. Holland failed to capitalize after that, and the dependable Gerd Müller shot West Germany ahead just before half-time. Sepp Maier performed brilliantly between the posts in the second half.

Star of the Tournament

A deceptively slight figure with a boyish face, Johan Cruyff was an unlikely soccer player. But his World Cup performances firmly established him as the driving force behind the Dutch team. Well suited to either a midfield or striking role, he was the complete embodiment of total soccer, inspiring his countrymen to new heights of international achievement. A year before the World Cup, Cruyff moved from Ajax, Amsterdam to Barcelona, where he spent four successful seasons. After a year of retirement, he sought a new challenge in the **North American Soccer League,** playing for the **Los Angeles Aztecs** and the **Washington Diplomats.**

1978

Argentina

The honor of staging a World Cup in Argentina, the birthplace of South American soccer, was long overdue. But political instability and unrest kept FIFA on tenterhooks throughout the competition. (FIFA's insecurities were especially justified in light of the assassination of the president of the tournament's organizing committee just two years before the big event.)

The finals were marked by increasingly dour, defensive soccer (perhaps because of the absence of the world's two best players, Johan Cruyff and Franz Beckenbauer) and inconsistent refereeing.

Memorable Matches

On the last day of second round matches, both Brazil and Argentina were still in contention for a place in the final. Brazil played first, beating Poland 3-1, thereby ensuring that Argentina would have to

win by at least four clear goals against Peru later that evening. Since Peru had beaten Scotland and tied Holland in the first round, it seemed like a tall order. But with the bit firmly between their teeth, the Argentinians rose to the challenge and stormed into attack. By the time the fourth goal had gone in, the Peruvians had completely fallen apart.

U.S. Spotlight

With more attention focused on the exploits of the U.S. national team than ever before, the Americans held their own against Mexico and Canada in the first round of qualifying play. All three teams finished with identical records, although Mexico's superior goal difference led them to win the group. Canada and the United States met in a play-off game in neutral Haiti, which Canada won easily, 3-0.

High & Low Points

In a bitter prelude to what proved to be a disastrous tournament for the Scots, winger **Willie Johnston** was sent home in disgrace after testing positive for taking amphetamines.

Tunisia demonstrated the increasing strength of African soccer by beating Mexico 3-0 and holding perennial power West Germany to a goalless draw. Only a narrow 1-0 loss to group winner Poland prevented the talented Tunisians from advancing to the second round.

Final: Argentina 3 Holland 1

Argentina got off to a shameful start by keeping the Dutch waiting five minutes before coming onto the confetti-showered field and then protesting the lightweight plaster cast on **René Van De Kerkhof's** arm. The referee did nothing about Argentina's intimidating tactics, and the Dutch responded in kind by committing 50 fouls during the match. An opportunistic goal by **Mario Kempes** put the Argentinians ahead, but Holland's famous "Clockwork Orange" finally got cranked up in the second half and **Dirk Nanninga** grabbed a much-deserved equalizing goal late in the match. Overtime and the World Cup, however, belonged to a revitalized Argentina, thanks to goals by Kempes and **Bertoni.**

Star of the Tournament

Four years after appearing in his first World Cup, Mario Kempes had been transformed from a gangly youngster into a fearsome striker. His graceful ball skills and devastating finishing plays brought him four goals in the first couple of rounds, including two crucial strikes against Peru. In a stroke of genius, Argentinian coach **Cesar Luis Menotti** moved him back into midfield in the latter stages of the tournament. He responded in the final with a virtuoso effort, scoring two goals and setting up the third.

Brazil has never failed to qualify for the World Cup finals. Even more impressive, it had never lost a single match in 63 years of World Cup qualifying play until its 2-0 defeat by Bolivia in 1993.

1982

Spain

The World Cup took another big step forward by expanding the number of teams in the finals from 16 to 24. Third world countries were the major beneficiaries, with the Africa, CONCACAF, and Asia/Oceania regions doubling their representatives to two each. China competed for the first time but lost out in the final round to Kuwait and New Zealand. New Zealand was forced to play a record 15 qualifying matches to ensure its place, including a 13-0 shellacking of Fiji, the biggest World Cup win ever. Meanwhile, Costa Rica sacrificed any chance of qualifying by refusing to travel to San Salvador for a match against El Salvador, citing the instability caused by the country's civil war. **Diego Maradona** made his World Cup debut. Unfortunately, like **Pelé** before him, he was shut down by the opposition.

Memorable Matches

Italy went into its decisive second match with Brazil still struggling to establish any form. The fact that Italy had even made it this far was amazing, considering it had failed to win a single match in the first round and had advanced only on the strength of scoring two goals to Cameroon's one. Brazil, however, seemed to be back to its attacking mode. What should have been a mismatch turned into a thrilling seesaw battle. **Paolo Rossi,** who had yet to score, pulled a hat trick while his opposite number **Serginho** missed a hatful of chances in Italy's 3-2 squeaker of a win.

A similar situation existed in the semi-final encounter between West Germany and France. The Germans had gotten off to a terrible start with a shocking 2-1 loss to Algeria, muddled through the next couple of rounds only to face a French side whose attacking brilliance had been the talk of the tournament. The first 90 minutes was marred by a violent foul on **Patrick Battiston** by German goalie **Harald "Toni" Schumacher** that left the French player unconscious. A penalty kick should have resolved what was then a 1-1 tie, but none was called and, incredibly, Schumacher remained on the field. In overtime, the French built a deserved 3-1 lead, but a controversial goal by **Karl-Heinz Rummenigge** put the Germans back into the match. Another goal tied the game at 3-3, thus forcing the World Cup's first penalty kick shootout, which was narrowly won by West Germany, 5-4.

U.S. Spotlight

Despite a 2-1 home win against Mexico, the United States still finished at the bottom of its qualifying group, due to a 5-1 loss in the return match in Mexico City, a goalless home draw with Canada, and a narrow 2-1 loss north of the border.

The maximum age for a World Cup referee is 45.

High & Low Points

Bryan Robson's goal for England after just 27 seconds into the first round match against France remains the quickest World Cup final score ever.

Northern Ireland's **Norman Whiteside,** at 17 years and 42 days old, became the youngest player to appear in a World Cup match, beating the "ageless" Pelé, who had made his debut when he was 17 years and 237 days old in 1958.

Hungary's record-tying 10-1 win against hapless El Salvador included a hat trick by substitute **Laszlo Kiss**—another World Cup first.

After West Germany had taken a 1-0 lead against Austria in the first round, the teams coasted the rest of the way, because both were guaranteed a place in the next round. Unfortunately for plucky Algeria, an identical record only led to a heartbreaking ouster because of its lower goal difference.

Final: Italy 3 W. Germany 1

Drained by its epic tussle with France, West Germany never got into a rhythm against Italy. The match became an anti-climax when Paolo Rossi gave Italy an early lead and the Germans' main offensive threat, Karl-Heinz Rummenigge, hobbled by injuries for the entire tournament, had to be substituted yet again. Goals by **Marco Tardelli** and **Allesandro Altobelli** iced an easy Italian victory, enabling veteran goalkeeper **Dino Zoff,** at 40, to become the oldest player to win a World Cup medal. West Germany's embarrassment was saved by a late **Paul Breitner** goal, but the team managed to miss a penalty shot—the first time ever in a final.

Star of the Tournament

Before the 1982 finals, concern was raised about Italy's lanky striker Paolo Rossi, who had just completed a two-year suspension for his role in a betting scandal with his club team—a charge he continues to strenuously deny. It was feared that Rossi would not be fit for such a major tournament. In Italy's first four games, he was held goalless and substituted twice. But in the game that really mattered, against mighty Brazil, Rossi notched a devastating hat trick. He then scored two goals in the semi-finals against Poland and the all-important opening goal against West Germany that set Italy on its way to the Cup itself. No other player that year bettered his record of six goals in three games.

1986

Mexico

Although Colombia had been the first choice to host the 1986 World Cup, its political instability and financial incapacity led FIFA to look elsewhere. A last-minute bid by the United States fell short and Brazil quickly dropped out of the running because of limited funds. This allowed Mexico—with its soccer infrastructure still in place from 1970—to become the first nation to hold the finals twice. As was the case in 1970, many matches were played in miserable conditions in midday heat and humidity. Compared to previous World Cups, it was a much more competitive tournament. One reason for this was the return to single-elimination matches in the second round rather than round-robin group play. Canada qualified, and Algeria surprised everyone by appearing in the finals for the second consecutive time.

Memorable Matches

Two of the most offensive-minded teams, France and Brazil, had the misfortune to meet in the quarter-finals, locking horns in a titanic struggle. In the first-half, **Careca's** goal for Brazil canceled out **Michel Platini's** effort for France, and that was the way it remained in regulation time, even though both teams swept up and down the field at will. The stalemated game of attractive, fluid soccer continued into the 30-minute overtime period, forcing another dreaded penalty kick shootout, which France won 4-3. But this was a match that neither team deserved to lose.

In fact, the only quarter-final settled without resorting to penalty kicks was Argentina against England. After a painfully slow start in the first round, England had been revived by striker **Gary Lineker.** After being shut out twice, his six goals in three matches won him the scoring title, emulating Paolo Rossi's feat four years earlier. Argentina, by contrast, had been steady yet unspectacular, but it exploded into life against England with one of the most controversial goals in World Cup history. From a cross to the far post, Argentina's fabled Diego Maradona rose high against English goalie **Peter Shilton** and "scored." Later he credited the goal to "the hand of God." Lineker quickly grabbed an equalizer, but as if to atone for his first effort, Maradona replied with one of the finest goals in World Cup history: a solo run in which he dribbled past four players, rounded Shilton, and calmly put the ball in the back of the net.

U.S. Spotlight

After easily disposing of Netherlands Antilles in the first qualifying round, the United States found the going much tougher against Costa Rica and Trinidad and Tobago in the second round. The Americans scored two narrow wins against Trinidad and Tobago, but a hard-earned 1-1 tie with Costa Rica in San José was followed by a heartbreaking 1-0 loss in Torrance, California. Costa Rica beat the United States by one point.

High & Low Points

Morocco became the first African nation ever to win a first-round group by way of two goalless draws against England and Poland and an outstanding 3-1 victory over Portugal. In the second round Morocco gave West Germany a scare before finally falling 1-0.

José Batista of Uruguay earned the dubious distinction of the quickest ejection in World Cup history: he was given his marching orders after only 55 seconds into the match against Scotland.

Final: Argentina 3
W. Germany 2

Argentina seemed to be on its way to a comfortable win, thanks to goals by **José Brown** and **Jorgé Valdano.** But West Germany had other ideas and in the final 17 minutes scored twice, through **Rudi Völler** and Karl-Heinz Rummenigge, to tie up the match. In an exciting battle of wits, Argentinian coach **Carlos Bilardo** took advantage of **Lothar Matthäus'** tight marking of Diego Maradona to pull his superstar back into midfield, thus defusing any offensive threat by the German skipper. In overtime Maradona supplied a picture-perfect pass to **Jorgé Burruchaga,** who strode downfield to draw out German goalie **Harald "Toni" Schumacher** before firing in the memorable winning goal.

Star of the Tournament

Diego Maradona had promised much but delivered very little in the 1982 World Cup. Heavily fouled by every team he faced, things finally boiled over when the stocky little forward was expelled for retaliating against Brazil. But in 1986, he finally lived up to his extravagant billing. Although his dynamic two goals against England proved crucial, it wasn't so much Maradona's goal scoring that made him such an awesome player, but his incredible dribbling skills and his totally unpredictable playmaking. Not a universally popular player in the Pelé mold, Maradona's image later suffered from drug problems and his boorish behavior in the 1990 World Cup.

▼▼▼▼▼▼

1990

Italy

Although the finals were once again dominated by the major soccer powers, clear signs appeared that lesser nations were beginning to catch up. Most impressive of all was Cameroon's reaching the quarter-finals—the first African team ever to do so. Africa's other representative, Egypt, also turned a few heads by holding Holland and Ireland to honorable draws and only losing narrowly to England. Costa Rica, under the masterful tutelage of

---

The weather had a tragic impact on a 1989 World Cup qualifying match between Nigeria and Angola. So intense was the heat that Nigerian star Sam Okwajari collapsed and died before proper medical attention could be administered. Thirteen fans in the stifling, overcrowded stadium also died as a result of the excessive temperature.

The television audience of 27.5 million for the 1990 World Cup semi-final match between Italy and Argentina made it the most widely watched program ever on Italian television. More than 87 percent of all sets in the country were tuned to the match.

Bora Milutinovich (now at the U.S. coaching helm), made it past the first round thanks to wins against Scotland and Sweden. The qualifying tournament was marred by a bizarre incident in the match between Brazil and Chile. A spectator in the Rio de Janeiro crowd threw a firecracker onto the field that allegedly felled Chilean goalkeeper **Roberto Rojas**. The Chilean team carried Rojas off the field and refused to restart the match. However, a FIFA investigation later revealed that Rojas had faked the whole thing. Brazil was awarded the game, Rojas was banned for life, and Chile was fined $31,000 and expelled from the 1994 World Cup.

Memorable Matches

From the moment Cameroon pulled off a huge upset 1-0 win against Argentina—the reigning world champions—in the first round, the "Indomitable Lions" were the talk of the tournament. Another win—2-1 against Romania—propelled the team to the top of its group and onto the second round, where it vanquished Colombia 2-1. The next hurdle was England in the quarter-finals. Thanks to another inspiring performance from **Roger Milla** (brought out of semi-retirement), Cameroon overcame a 1-0 half-time deficit with two well-deserved goals only to rashly concede a penalty, sending the match into overtime. A second penalty, converted once more by the dependable Gary Lineker, sealed Cameroon's fate while the crowd witnessed the underdog's last incredible ride of World Cup play.

England's semi-final opponent was a rampant West Germany, which quickly jumped to a 1-0 lead thanks to a deflected **Andreas Brehme** free-kick that caught goalie **Peter Shilton** uncharacteristically out of position. But with midfielder **Paul Gascoigne** spurring on his English teammates, Gary Lineker, at his opportunistic best, snapped up an equalizer nine minutes from the game's end. The game ultimately went to penalty kicks, during which **Chris Waddle** shot high over the bar, giving the West Germans a dramatic 4-3 triumph.

U.S. Spotlight

After a goalless first match, the United States rolled over Jamaica in a 5-1 rout that sent it into the final qualifying round. A split with Costa Rica, a 1-1 home tie with Trinidad and Tobago, and a win and a tie against both El Salvador and Guatemala set up a crucial match for the Americans in Port of Spain. Needing a win to guarantee a trip to Italy, the United States stunned Trinidad and Tobago with a scorching 40-yarder by **Paul Caligiuri** and saw to it that the goal held up for the rest of the game. An inexperienced U.S. team, appearing in its first finals in 40 years, received a fiery baptism with a 5-1 hammering from Czechoslovakia—another magnificent Caligiuri goal had pegged the score at 2-1, providing a flicker of hope—but salvaged a lot of pride by more than holding its own against Italy, only succumbing 1-0. The United States exited the first round with a disappointing 2-1 loss to Austria—a team reduced to 10 men in the first half—but **Bruce Murray's** late goal offered at least a little consolation.

High & Low Points

Italian goalkeeper **Walter Zenga** established a World Cup record by going 517 minutes without conceding a goal. He kept opponents at bay through all three first-round matches, the second round encounter with Uruguay, and the quarter-final against Ireland. Finally, Argentina's **Claudio Caniggia** got the ball past Zenga in the 67th minute of the semi-final; ironically, Argentina then put four goals past Zenga and won the penalty kick shootout, 4-3.

There was major disappointment, not to mention embarrassment, for another goalie, **René Higuita** of Colombia, who had become famous for his constant forays outside the penalty area, where he liked to show off his "sweeper" skills. He was badly caught out of position in quarter-final overtime when Cameroon's crafty **Roger Milla** stripped the ball from him and calmly rolled in the winning goal.

The overall tally of 164 yellow cards and 16 red cards issued by busy referees during the tournament was the most ever in a World Cup.

Final: W. Germany 1
Argentina 0

In the course of getting to the final, Argentina racked up 22 bookings and three ejections, resulting in the suspension of four of its prime players (most notably Claudio Caniggia) for the crucial match. Up to this point the Argentinians had been somewhat cautious, relying on penalty kick shootouts to beat Italy and Yugoslavia in the previous rounds. But against West Germany it became downright negative. Repeated German attacks could find no way around a packed Argentinian defense. Thirty minutes from the end, with the match becoming increasingly tense, **Pedro Monzon** was ejected for a heavy foul on **Jurgen Klinsmann**. Things degenerated from there, until, with five minutes to go, **Roberto Sensini** brought down **Rudi Völler**, and Brehme scored from the penalty spot. **Gustavo Dezotti** received his marching orders for wrestling Klinsmann to the ground, and after the match a tearful Diego Maradona refused to shake FIFA President **João Havelange's** hand. West Germany, coached by the same Franz Beckenbauer who had captained its 1974 World Cup winning team, had exacted revenge for its loss to Argentina four years earlier, but it had been unquestionably the worst World Cup final ever.

Star of the Tournament

West Germany's Lothar Matthäus made his presence felt on the 1990 World Cup from his country's very first match against Yugoslavia, when the elegant midfielder got himself on the score-sheet twice. His second effort, a 40-yard dribbling run followed by a 30-yard rocket-shot, was widely recognized as the best goal of the tournament. Two more goals—including a penalty winner against Czechoslovakia in the quarter-finals—plus his relentless running and pinpoint passing, firmly established Matthäus as the guiding force behind an outstanding West German team.

Glossary of Soccer Terms

A

Advantage rule A law enabling the referee to choose not to stop a match and penalize a player for an offense if the referee feels it will actually help the offending team.

AFC See **Asian Football Association.**

Aggregate score Total score from a home-and-away series in a single-elimination tournament. For example, if the score is United States 3 Canada 1, and Canada 2 United States 1, the United States would win by an aggregate score of 4 to 3.

American Professional Soccer League (APSL) A U.S. league formed in 1990 after a merger of the American Soccer League and the Western Soccer League.

Asian Football Association (AFC) Soccer confederation of Asian countries.

B

Banana kick Kicking the ball to make it swerve, bend, or spin.

Bicycle kick A dramatic overhead kick.

Booking When a referee writes down the name of a player who's been given a caution.

Bundesliga Germany's first-division soccer league.

C

CAF See **Confédération Africaine de Football.**

Catenaccio A tactical formation that originated in Italy using at least five defenders. Literally, the Italian word means "great chain."

Caution An official warning given to a player who violates the laws of the game, indicated by the referee holding up a yellow card. Two cautions result in a red card and an ejection.

Center See **Cross.**

Charging Making physical contact with an opponent in a violent or dangerous manner. However, leaning one's shoulder against an opponent's shoulder (with arms and elbows tucked in) is permitted as a fair charge, provided that the ball is within playing distance. The penalty for charging is a direct free kick.

Chip Lofting the ball over an opponent's head.

Clear Moving the ball downfield, usually as a means of relieving pressure from the opposing team's attacks.

CONCACAF See **Confederación Norte-Centroamericana y del Fútbol.**

Confederación Norte-Centroamericana y del Fútbol (CONCACAF) Soccer confederation of North American, Central American, and Caribbean countries.

Confederación Sudamericana de Fútbol (CONMEBOL) Soccer confederation of South America.

Confédération Africaine de Football (CAF) Soccer confederation of African countries.

CONMEBOL See **Confederación Sudamericana de Fútbol.**

Copa América A single-elimination tournament for CONMEBOL nations held every two years. The Copa was expanded in 1993 to include select CONCACAF nations.

Copa Libertadores A single-elimination tournament for CONMEBOL's best club teams, held annually.

Corner kick A procedure used to put the ball back into play after it is sent across the goal line by the defending team. The attacking team kicks the ball onto the field from the corner arc on the side where it went out of play.

Crossbar The horizontal bar that connects the goalpost.

Cross An aerial kick into the penalty area from near the touchline (to cross the ball is also known as centering).

D

Dangerous play Any action by a player against an opponent that in the referee's opinion endangers the safety of the opponent, such as high kicking a ball close to an opponent's head or attempting to kick a ball held by the opposing goalkeeper. The penalty for dangerous play is an indirect free kick.

Dead ball A ball that is not in play because it has completely crossed either the goal line or the touchline, or because the referee has stopped play for some reason.

Defenders Players positioned at the back of the field whose main job is to prevent the opposition from scoring. Most teams have four defenders, including two **fullbacks,** a **stopper,** and a **sweeper.**

Diagonal run Moving diagonally across the field into open space to receive a pass.

Direct free kick A free kick from which a player can score a goal without another player having to touch the ball.

Draw A tie.

Dribbling Controlling and protecting the ball while moving it downfield using both feet.

Drop ball A procedure used to put the ball back into play when a match has been interrupted by an injury or a substitution, or when it's difficult to determine which team put the ball out of bounds. One player from each team faces off at the point where the incident occurred, and the referee drops the ball between them. The ball can be played as soon as it hits the ground.

India withdrew from the 1950 World Cup when FIFA refused a request to allow its players to compete barefoot.

Dummy A trick play used to fool an opponent so that instead of trapping the ball, a player lets it go through his or her legs to a better-placed teammate.

 E

Equalizer A goal that ties the score.

European Championship A single-elimination tournament for the UEFA countries, held every four years.

European Cup A single-elimination tournament for winners of the league championship in each UEFA-member country, held annually.

European Cup Winners Cup A single-elimination tournament for winners of the cup competition held in each UEFA-member country, held annually.

 F

F.A. Cup (Football Association Cup) First single-elimination tournament of its kind, for English club teams, held annually.

Far post Goal post farthest from the ball.

Fédération Internationale de Football Association (FIFA) Soccer's international governing body.

Feinting Faking a play to fool an opponent.

FIFA See **Fédération Internationale de Football Association.**

Forwards Attacking players on the front line of a team who are responsible for scoring most of the goals. Types of forwards include **strikers** and **wingers.** Most teams have no more than three forwards.

Foul An offense violating the laws of the game and resulting in the award of a direct or indirect free kick for the team that is the victim of the foul.

Free kick An opportunity awarded to a team, when one of its players is seriously fouled or another major offense is committed by the opposing team. The ball is kicked back into play from the point at which the foul or offense took place. There are two forms of free kicks: direct and indirect.

Friendly An exhibition match.

Fullbacks Defenders positioned on the right or left flanks in the defensive line directly in front of the goalkeeper whose main task is to guard against opponents attacking their particular side.

 G

Goal The 8-foot-high and 8-yard-wide target into which players attempt to get the ball to score in soccer. Also, when a ball goes under the crossbar, between the goal posts, and completely across the goal line, resulting in a team scoring.

Goal area The 20-by-6-yard area directly in front of the goal.

Goal difference The difference between the number of goals a team scores and the number it concedes.

Goalkeeper The player who defends the goal. Also known as the goalie, this is the only player, other than players taking throw-ins, allowed to use his or her hands.

Goal kick An indirect free kick whereby the ball is put back into play after it has been sent across the goal line by the attacking team. The defending team can kick the ball from anywhere in the goal area on the side where it went out of play.

Goal line The end line running from one corner of the field to the other and connecting the touchlines.

Gold Cup A single-elimination tournament for CONCACAF countries, held every two years.

 H

Half volley Kicking the ball as it hits the ground.

Hand ball Intentional touching of the ball with any part of the arm (except to take a throw-in) by any player other than the goalkeeper. The penalty for handing the ball is a direct free kick.

Hat trick The scoring of three goals in a single game.

Heading Using the head to propel or control the ball.

Home-and-away series A two-match series in which each team plays one game on their home field and the other (the "away" match) on their opponents' field.

 I

Indirect free kick A free kick from which the kicker's team can score a goal only after another player (aside from the kicker) touches the ball.

Injury Time Time added to the end of a match at the discretion of the referee because of injuries, time-wasting, and substitutions.

International Football Association Board The administrative body that revises and changes the laws of the game.

 J

Jockeying Responding to an opponent's every move, while cutting off his or her most direct route to the goal.

 K

Kick-off The way in which the ball is put into play to start each half of a match, to restart a game after a goal is scored, or to start each half of an overtime period. The ball is placed on the center spot and kicked into the opponents' half of the field.

L

Laws of the Game The official rules of soccer, as decided by the International Football Association Board.

League soccer A championship based on round-robin play.

Libero Italian term for a sweeper.

Linesmen Two officials who assist the referee by signaling when the ball goes out of play or when offside or other infractions occur.

  M

Manager Coach.

Marking Guarding an opponent.

Midfielders Players positioned in the center of the field who provide the link between defenders and forwards. They receive the ball from defenders and are then responsible for moving it downfield and setting it up for forwards. Most teams have three to five midfielders.

  N

NASL See **North American Soccer League.**

National Team The team selected to represent a country, usually composed of its best players.

Near post The goal post closest to the ball.

North American Soccer League (NASL) The defunct professional soccer league in the United States and Canada, in operation from 1968 to 1985.

Nutmeg Moving past an opponent by kicking the ball through his or her legs.

  O

Obstruction Deliberately blocking the path of an opponent to prevent him or her from playing the ball. Obstruction is penalized with an indirect free kick unless the ball is within playing distance.

Oceania Football Confederation (OFC) Soccer confederation of Oceanic countries.

OFC See **Oceania Football Confederation.**

Offside An offense that occurs when a player is closer to the opponents' goal line than the ball at the time the ball was last played, except when the player is in his or her own half of the field; there are two opponents closer to their own goal than the player; the ball was last touched by the opponent or last played by the player; or the player received the ball from a goal kick, corner kick, throw-in, or drop ball. If the player is in an offside position but isn't interfering with play, he or she isn't considered offside. An offside call results in an indirect free kick for the opposing team at the point where the player was called offside.

Offside trap A means of catching an opposing team offside by moving forward at the split second an opponent plays the ball forward to a teammate.

Olympic Soccer Tournament A single-elimination tournament for the world's top players under the age of 23, held every four years during the summer games.

One-touch Passing, shooting, or heading the ball in one fluid movement, without attempting to trap it.

Overlapping An attacking movement by a defender, usually down the flanks.

Over the top An illegal tackle when a player goes "over the top" of the ball and deliberately kicks an opponent's leg.

Own goal An accidental goal scored by a player who inadvertently puts the ball into the goal he or she is defending.

 P

Passing Moving the ball from one player to another.

Penalty area The 18-by-44-yard area in front of the goal in which the goalkeeper is allowed to handle the ball.

Penalty kick When a player commits a direct free kick violation within his or her own penalty area, a player for the team that was fouled takes an unimpeded shot at the opposing goalkeeper from the penalty spot.

Penalty kick shootout A way of settling a tied game when overtime doesn't result in a winner. Each team nominates five players, who in turn take a penalty kick against the opposing goalkeeper. If the score still remains tied after the fifth round, alternate penalty kicks, one for each team, are taken until a winner is determined.

Pitch British word for a soccer field.

Professional foul A deliberate and planned foul against an opponent to deny him or her a clear goal-scoring opportunity. The guilty player may be ejected from the game by the referee.

 R

Red Card A red card held up by the referee to indicate the ejection of a player from the match.

Referee A person given the authority to officiate a soccer match.

Running off the ball Moving around the field without the ball with the purpose of getting into an open position from which to receive the ball.

The word "soccer" came into use in the 1880s at Oxford and Cambridge to disassociate it from rugby. It was an abbreviated version of the term "association football," itself derived from the appellation of the Football Association in England, formed in 1863.

S

Save When the goalkeeper catches or deflects the ball to prevent a goal from being scored.

Serie A Italy's first-division soccer league.

Set plays Pre-established plays such as throw-ins, corner kicks, free kicks, and penalty kicks that are the only predictable elements in a sport that is largely unprogrammed.

Shooting Kicking the ball deliberately in an attempt to score a goal.

Side Team.

Stopper A defender positioned in the middle of the defensive line in front of the goalkeeper who usually guards the opposing team's most dangerous striker.

Striker A forward who concentrates on scoring goals.

Supercopa A single-elimination tournament for previous winners of the Copa Libertadores, held annually.

Sweeper A defender who moves freely around the field to guard against attacking opponents who have made it past the other defenders.

  T

Tackling Taking the ball away from an opponent.

Through pass A pass into open space behind an opposing team's line of defenders for the intended recipient to run to.

Throw-in A set play where the ball is thrown back into play from the point where it crossed the touchline by either team. The team that didn't touch the ball last takes the throw-in.

Time-wasting Delaying the game after the ball is dead.

Total soccer When all members on a team have the tactical ability to play offense, midfield, and defense interchangeably.

Touchline Sideline on a soccer field.

Trapping Bringing the ball under control by stopping it with the foot, thigh, chest, or head.

 U

UEFA See **Union of European Football Association.**

UEFA Cup An annual, single-elimination tournament for the best teams from the UEFA-member countries that do not participate in the European Cup or the European Cup Winners Cup.

Under-17 World Cup An international soccer tournament for the world's top players under the age of 17, held every two years.

Under-20 World Cup An international soccer tournament for the world's top players under the age of 20, held every two years.

Union of European Football Association (UEFA) Soccer confederation of European countries.

U.S. Cup An annual round-robin tournament matching the United States with some of the world's top soccer nations.

U.S. Soccer The governing body of soccer in the United States.

   V

Volleying Kicking the ball in midair.

 W

Wall A line of players used to defend against a free kick.

Wall pass A pass from one player to another in which the second player, acting as a wall, directs the ball with one touch back to his or her teammate.

Winger A forward positioned close to the touchline who tries to get around the opposing defense to feed the ball to the strikers or to score.

Women's World Cup An international soccer tournament for the top women's national teams, held every four years.

World Cup The world's largest international soccer tournament, open to the national team of every country that is a member of the FIFA, held every four years.

World Cup final The championship game of the World Cup, played by the two teams that make it through the month-long finals tournament.

World Cup finals The month-long World Cup tournament played by the 24 nations that make it through the 18-month-long qualifying tournament.

 Y

Yellow Card A yellow card held up by the referee to indicate a caution.

  Z

Zone Defense A strategy whereby players guard a part of the field rather than a specific opponent.

In 1976, a soccer-mad couple in Walsall, England, decided to name their newborn son after all the members of the Manchester United team that had made it through to the English Football Association Cup final that year—15 years later Graham Alex Jimmy Stewart Gerry Brian Martin Steve Sammy Stuart Lou Gordon David Tommy Matt Cross was signed by Leeds United, one of Manchester United's biggest rivals.

Page

ACCESS® Notes

Page

Page

ACCESS® Notes

Page

ACCESS® Notes

Page

ACCESS® Guides

Please send me the following **ACCESS**® Guides:

☐ **BARCELONA**ACCESS® $17.00
0-06-277000-4

☐ **BOSTON**ACCESS® $18.00
0-06-277049-7

☐ **CARIBBEAN**ACCESS® $17.00
0-06-277042-X

☐ **CHICAGO**ACCESS® $18.00
0-06-277048-9

☐ **FLORENCE/VENICE/ MILAN**ACCESS® $17.00
0-06-277001-2

☐ **HAWAII**ACCESS® $18.00
0-06-277068-3

☐ **LAS VEGAS**ACCESS® $18.00 (available 12/93)
0-06-277055-1

☐ **LONDON**ACCESS® $18.00
0-06-277051-9

☐ **LOS ANGELES**ACCESS® $18.00
0-06-277047-0

☐ **MEXICO**ACCESS® $17.00
0-06-277041-1

☐ **MIAMI & SOUTH FLORIDA**ACCESS® $18.00
0-06-277070-5

☐ **NEW YORK CITY**ACCESS® $18.00
0-06-277052-7

☐ **ORLANDO & CENTRAL FLORIDA**ACCESS® $18.00
0-06-277069-1

☐ **PARIS**ACCESS® $18.00
0-06-277038-1

☐ **ROME**ACCESS® $18.00
0-06-277053-5

☐ **SAN DIEGO**ACCESS® $18.00
0-06-277004-7

☐ **SAN FRANCISCO**ACCESS® $18.00
0-06-277046-2

☐ **SANTA FE/TAOS/ ALBUQUERQUE**ACCESS® $18.00
0-06-277054-3

☐ **SEATTLE**ACCESS® $18.00
0-06-277050-0

☐ **SKI COUNTRY**ACCESS® Western United States $18.00
0-06-277066-7

☐ **SOCCER**ACCESS® $12.00
0-06-277107-8

☐ **THE WALL STREET JOURNAL** Guide to Understanding Money & Markets $13.95
0-06-772516-3

☐ **WASHINGTON DC**ACCESS® $18.00
0-06-277039-X

☐ **WINE COUNTRY**ACCESS® Northern California $18.00
0-06-277006-3

Prices subject to change without notice.

Total for **ACCESS**® Guides:	$
Please add applicable sales tax:	
Add $4.00 for first book S&H, $1.00 per additional book:	
Total payment:	$